AFGHANS

FOR ALL SEASONS • BOOK 3

*E*ach season has its own simple pleasures. Spring brings the earth's renewal with green grass and bouquets of flowers, while summer invites us to come out and play in the cheerful sunshine. Autumn offers a kaleidoscope of colors with its changing leaves, and winter allows us to settle in and enjoy the company of friends and family. Whatever each season holds for you, this collection of 52 cover-ups will take you through the year in comfort and style. From light-and-lacy springtime throws to thick-and-toasty winter wraps, the creations in this book are sure to please and also make perfect gifts for those you love. No matter what your skill level — whether you're a beginner or an advanced crocheter — you can count on Leisure Arts to provide simple-to-follow instructions, full-color photography, and helpful diagrams to aid you every step of the way. So choose your favorites now and start crocheting your way through the seasons!

LEISURE ARTS, INC., and OXMOOR HOUSE, INC.

Afghans For All Seasons, Book 3
Published by Leisure Arts, Inc., and Oxmoor House, Inc.

Hardcover ISBN 1-57486-258-8
Softcover ISBN 1-57486-257-X

10 9 8 7 6 5 4 3 2

TABLE OF CONTENTS

SPRING 4

Cobblestone Path 6
Meadow 8
Stunning Stripes 10
Spring Fancy 12
Viola Patch 14
Soft Clover 17
Floral Bounty 20
Lullaby 22
Enchantment 25
Veranda 28
Blushing Beauty 30
Reverie 32
Picturesque Posies 34

SUMMER 38

Sunrise 40
American Spirit 42
Bride's Dream 44
Lavender & Lace 46
Star-Spangled Banner 48
Tropical Delight 51
Elegant Ivy 54
Idyllic Day 56
Pretty in Pink 58
Vibrant Visions 61
Carnival 64
Rosy Comfort 66
Dazzling Dahlias 68

AUTUMN 70

Harvest Blend 72
Thanksgiving 74
Spiced Tea 76
Rock-A-Bye Blanket 78
Log Cabin Legacy 80
Home on the Range 82
Sun-Baked Tiles 85
Autumn Glory 88
Hospitality 90
Fall Festival 93
Remnants 96
Mums Galore 98
Fall Breeze 100

WINTER 102

Memories 104
Snow on the Pines 106
Cozy Classic 108
Hearthside Stripes 110
Angels All Around 112
Chill Chaser 115
Tradition 118
Pretty Poinsettias 120
Icicles 123
Fireside Companion 126
Christmas Crowns 128
Warm & Cuddly 131
Winter Melody 134

General Instructions 136
Credits 143

SPRING

*As Mother Nature wakes from her winter-long
slumber, the earth takes on new life! There's an air of
excitement that naturally seems to stir our creativity. What
better time to crochet light-and-breezy afghans for your home
or to share with others? Worked in the refreshing colors
of spring, this collection of cover-ups symbolizes the
things that make the season so rejuvenating.*

Cobblestone Path

This captivating cobblestone path leads to comfort! The blanket is worked in strips, making it a "walk in the park" to crochet.

Finished Size: 45¹/₂" x 59"

MATERIALS
Worsted Weight Yarn:
 Ecru - 31 ounces, (880 grams, 2,020 yards)
 Rose - 10¹/₂ ounces, (300 grams, 685 yards)
Crochet hook, size J (6.00 mm) **or** size needed for gauge
Yarn needle

GAUGE: Each Strip = 6¹/₂" wide

Gauge Swatch: 4"w x 3³/₄"h
Work same as Center through Row 6.

STITCH GUIDE

FRONT POST HALF DOUBLE CROCHET
 (abbreviated FPhdc)
YO, insert hook from **front** to **back** around post of FPtr indicated *(Fig. 10, page 139)*, YO and pull up a loop, YO and draw through all 3 loops on hook. Skip st behind FPhdc.

FRONT POST DOUBLE CROCHET
 (abbreviated FPdc)
YO, insert hook from **front** to **back** around post of st indicated *(Fig. 10, page 139)*, YO and pull up a loop (3 loops on hook), (YO and draw through 2 loops on hook) twice. Skip st behind FPdc.

FRONT POST TREBLE CROCHET
 (abbreviated FPtr)
YO twice, insert hook from **front** to **back** around post of st indicated *(Fig. 10, page 139)*, YO and pull up a loop (4 loops on hook), (YO and draw through 2 loops on hook) 3 times. Skip st behind FPtr.

STRIP (Make 7)
CENTER
With Ecru, ch 17 **loosely**.
Row 1: Dc in fourth ch from hook **(3 skipped chs count as first dc)** and in each ch across: 15 dc.
Row 2 (Right side): Ch 3 **(counts as first dc, now and throughout)**, turn; ★ dc in next dc, skip next dc, work 3 FPtr around next dc, skip next dc; repeat from ★ 2 times **more**, dc in last 2 dc.

Note: Loop a short piece of yarn around any stitch to mark Row 2 as **right** side and bottom edge.
Row 3: Ch 3, turn; work FPdc around next dc and around each st across.
Row 4: Ch 3, turn; ★ dc in next FPdc, skip next FPdc, work 3 FPtr around next FPdc, skip next FPdc; repeat from ★ 2 times **more**, dc in last 2 sts.
Rows 5-92: Repeat Rows 3 and 4, 44 times.
Finish off.

BORDER
Rnd 1: With **right** side facing and working in end of rows, join Rose with slip st in Row 1; ch 4 **(counts as first dc plus ch 1)**, dc in same row, 2 dc in next row and in each row across to last row, (dc, ch 1, dc) twice in last row; working across sts on Row 92, skip first 3 sts, work FPtr around next FPtr, † skip next FPtr, 3 tr in next dc, skip next FPtr, work FPtr around next FPtr †; repeat from † to † once **more**, skip next 3 sts; working in end of rows, (dc, ch 1, dc) twice in first row, 2 dc in next row and in each row across to last row, (dc, ch 1, dc) twice in last row; working around sts on Row 1 and in free loops of beginning ch *(Fig. 17b, page 141)*, skip first 3 dc, work FPtr around next dc, ★ skip next ch, 3 tr in next ch, skip next ch, work FPtr around next dc; repeat from ★ once **more**, skip last 3 chs, (dc, ch 1, dc) in end of same row as first dc; join with slip st to first dc, finish off: 394 sts.
Rnd 2: With **right** side facing, join Ecru with slip st in first ch-1 sp; ch 2 **(counts as first hdc)**, hdc in same sp, † (skip next 2 dc, 2 hdc in sp **before** next dc) 90 times, 2 hdc in next ch-1 sp, 6 dc in next ch-1 sp, work FPtr around next FPtr, ★ skip next tr, 5 tr in next tr, skip next tr, work FPtr around next FPtr; repeat from ★ once **more**, 6 dc in next ch-1 sp †, 2 hdc in next ch-1 sp, repeat from † to † once; join with slip st to first hdc, finish off.
Rnd 3: With **right** side facing and working in Back Loops Only *(Fig. 16, page 141)*, join Rose with sc in same st as joining *(see Joining With Sc, page 140)*; place marker around sc just made for joining placement, † sc in next hdc and in each hdc across to next corner 6-dc group, place marker around last sc made for joining placement, sc in next 6 dc, work

2 FPhdc around next FPtr, (sc in next 5 tr, work
2 FPhdc around next FPtr) twice †, sc in next 7 sts,
place marker around last sc made for joining
placement, repeat from † to † once, sc in last 6 dc;
join with slip st to **both** loops of first sc, finish off.

ASSEMBLY

With Rose and working through inside loops only,
whipstitch long edge of Strips together *(Fig. 21a,
page 142)*, beginning in first marked sc and ending
in next marked sc.

Meadow

Worked in a mossy green hue, this inviting cover-up resembles a beautiful meadow.
Stitch up this design of clusters and scallops to bring the wonder of nature indoors.

Finished Size: 49" x 65"

MATERIALS
Worsted Weight Yarn:
30 ounces, (850 grams, 1,970 yards)
Crochet hook, size I (5.50 mm) **or** size needed for gauge

GAUGE: In pattern,
sc, (work Cluster, sc) 3 times and
Rows 1-6 = $3^1/4$"

STITCH GUIDE

CLUSTER
Ch 3, YO, insert hook in third ch from hook, YO and pull up a loop, YO and draw through 2 loops on hook, YO, insert hook in same ch, YO and pull up a loop, YO and draw through 2 loops on hook, YO and draw through all 3 loops on hook (*Figs. 11a & b, page 139*).
SCALLOP
Ch 3, dc in third ch from hook.

AFGHAN BODY

Ch 198 **loosely**.

Row 1: Sc in second ch from hook, ★ work Cluster, skip next 3 chs, sc in next ch; repeat from ★ across: 49 Clusters.

Row 2 (Right side): Ch 5 **(counts as first tr plus ch 1, now and throughout unless otherwise indicated)**, turn; sc in next Cluster (ch-3 sp), work Cluster, sc in next Cluster, ch 4, sc in next Cluster, ★ (work Cluster, sc in next Cluster) twice, ch 4, sc in next Cluster; repeat from ★ across to last Cluster, work Cluster, sc in last Cluster, ch 1, tr in last sc: 32 Clusters.

Row 3: Ch 1, turn; sc in first tr, work Cluster, ★ sc in next Cluster, ch 4, sc in next ch-4 sp, ch 4, sc in next Cluster, work Cluster; repeat from ★ across to last tr, sc in last tr: 17 Clusters.

Row 4: Ch 5, turn; sc in next Cluster, ★ ch 4, (sc in next ch-4 sp, ch 4) twice, sc in next Cluster; repeat from ★ across to last sc, ch 1, tr in last sc: 48 ch-4 sps.

Row 5: Ch 1, turn; sc in first tr, work Cluster, ★ sc in next ch-4 sp, (ch 4, sc in next ch-4 sp) twice, work Cluster; repeat from ★ across to last tr, sc in last tr: 17 Clusters.

Row 6: Ch 5, turn; sc in next Cluster, ★ work Cluster, sc in next ch-4 sp, ch 4, sc in next ch-4 sp, work Cluster, sc in next Cluster; repeat from ★ across to last sc, ch 1, tr in last sc: 32 Clusters.

Row 7: Ch 1, turn; sc in first tr, work Cluster, sc in next Cluster, work Cluster, sc in next ch-4 sp, work Cluster, ★ (sc in next Cluster, work Cluster) twice, sc in next ch-4 sp, work Cluster; repeat from ★ across to last Cluster, sc in last Cluster, work Cluster, sc in last tr: 49 Clusters.

Row 8: Ch 5, turn; sc in next Cluster, work Cluster, sc in next Cluster, ch 4, sc in next Cluster, ★ (work Cluster, sc in next Cluster) twice, ch 4, sc in next Cluster; repeat from ★ across to last Cluster, work Cluster, sc in last Cluster, ch 1, tr in last sc: 32 Clusters.

Rows 9-127: Repeat Rows 3-8, 19 times; then repeat Rows 3-7 once **more**.

Row 128: Ch 5 **(counts as first hdc plus ch 3)**, turn; skip first Cluster, hdc in next sc, ★ ch 3, skip next Cluster, hdc in next sc; repeat from ★ across, do **not** finish off.

EDGING

Do **not** turn; work Scallop; working in end of rows, skip first 2 rows, ★ slip st around tr on next row, work Scallop, skip next row; repeat from ★ across; working in free loops (*Fig. 17b, page 141*) and in sps across beginning ch, slip st in ch at base of first sc, work Scallop, (slip st in next sp, work Scallop) across to last ch, slip st in last ch, work Scallop; working in end of rows, skip first row, slip st around tr on next row, work Scallop, † skip next row, slip st around tr on next row, work Scallop †; repeat from † to † across to last 2 rows, skip last 2 rows; working across Row 128, slip st in first hdc, work Scallop, (slip st in next ch-3 sp, work Scallop) across to last hdc, slip st in last hdc; finish off.

Stunning Stripes

This stunningly striped afghan will brighten any room with a refreshing burst of color. Each row is worked across the length of the afghan.

Finished Size: 46¹/₂" x 62"

MATERIALS
Worsted Weight Yarn:
    Ecru - 16 ounces, (450 grams, 905 yards)
    Lt Plum - 16 ounces, (450 grams, 905 yards)
    Lt Green - 14 ounces, (400 grams, 790 yards)
    Dk Plum - 9 ounces, (260 grams, 510 yards)
    Dk Green - 7 ounces, (200 grams, 395 yards)
Crochet hook, size I (5.50 mm) **or** size needed
    for gauge

GAUGE: In pattern, 10 sts and 8 rows = 3"

Gauge Swatch: 3¹/₄"w x 3"h
With Ecru, ch 12 **loosely**.
Work same as Afghan Body for 8 rows.

STITCH GUIDE

FRONT POST DOUBLE CROCHET
  (abbreviated FPdc)
YO, insert hook from **front** to **back** around post
of dc indicated *(Fig. 10, page 139)*, YO and pull
up a loop (3 loops on hook), (YO and draw
through 2 loops on hook) twice.

COLOR SEQUENCE
2 Rows **each**: ★ † Ecru, Lt Plum, Dk Plum, Lt Plum,
Ecru †, Lt Green, Dk Green, Lt Green; repeat from ★
6 times **more**, then repeat from † to † once.

*Note: Each row is worked across length of Afghan.
When joining yarn and finishing off, leave an 8" end
to be worked into fringe.*

AFGHAN BODY
With Ecru, ch 208 **loosely**.
Row 1 (Wrong side): Sc in second ch from hook, (dc
in next ch, sc in next ch) across; finish off: 207 sts.
*Note: Loop a short piece of yarn around **back** of any
stitch on Row 1 to mark **right** side.*

Row 2: With **right** side facing, join Ecru with slip st
in first sc; ch 2 **(counts as first hdc, now and
throughout)**, work FPdc around next dc, (sc in next
sc, work FPdc around next dc) across to last sc, hdc
in last sc; finish off.
Row 3: With **wrong** side facing, join next color with
sc in first hdc *(see Joining With Sc, page 140)*; (sc in
next FPdc, dc in next sc) across to last 2 sts, sc in last
2 sts; finish off.
Row 4: With **right** side facing, join same color with
slip st in first sc; ch 2, sc in next sc, (work FPdc
around next dc, sc in next sc) across to last sc, hdc in
last sc; finish off.
Row 5: With **wrong** side facing, join next color with
sc in first hdc; dc in next sc, (sc in next FPdc, dc in
next sc) across to last hdc, sc in last hdc; finish off.
Row 6: With **right** side facing, join same color with
slip st in first sc; ch 2, work FPdc around next dc, (sc
in next sc, work FPdc around next dc) across to last
sc, hdc in last sc; finish off.
Rows 7-122: Repeat Rows 3-6, 29 times.

TRIM
FIRST SIDE
Row 1: With **wrong** side facing, join Ecru with sc in
first hdc on Row 122; sc in next FPdc, ch 1, ★ skip
next sc, sc in next FPdc, ch 1; repeat from ★ across to
last 3 sts, skip next sc, sc in last 2 sts; finish off.
Row 2: With **right** side facing, join Ecru with slip st
in first sc; ch 2, (slip st in next ch-1 sp, ch 2) across to
last 2 sc, skip next sc, slip st in last sc; finish off.

SECOND SIDE
Row 1: With **wrong** side facing and working in free
loops of beginning ch *(Fig. 17b, page 141)*, join Ecru
with sc in first ch; sc in next ch, ch 1, ★ skip next ch,
sc in next ch, ch 1; repeat from ★ across to chs at
base of last 3 sts, skip next ch, sc in next 2 chs;
finish off.
Row 2: With **right** side facing, join Ecru with slip st
in first sc; ch 2, (slip st in next ch-1 sp, ch 2) across to
last 2 sc, skip next sc, slip st in last sc; finish off.

Holding 2 strands of corresponding color yarn
together, each 17" long, add additional fringe in each
row across short edges of Afghan *(Figs. 22b & d,
page 142)*.

Spring Fancy

You'll strike everyone's fancy with our lacy afghan. The lightweight pattern of picots lends the throw its eye-catching appeal.

Finished Size: 50" x 65¹/₂"

MATERIALS
Worsted Weight Yarn:
47 ounces, (1,330 grams, 2,270 yards)
Crochet hook, size I (5.50 mm) **or** size needed for gauge

GAUGE: In pattern, 2 repeats = 4";
6 rows = 3"

Gauge Swatch: 4¹/₄"w x 3¹/₂"h
Ch 18.
Work same as Afghan Body for 7 rows.
Finish off.

STITCH GUIDE

PICOT
Ch 3, sc in third ch from hook.
DECREASE (uses next 7 sts)
YO, skip next dc, insert hook in next dc, YO and pull up a loop, YO and draw through 2 loops on hook, YO, skip next 4 sts, insert hook in next dc, YO and pull up a loop, YO and draw through 2 loops on hook, YO and draw through all 3 loops on hook.

AFGHAN BODY

Ch 154, place marker in second ch from hook for st placement.
Row 1 (Right side): Working in back ridges of beginning ch *(Fig. 2b, page 137)*, sc in second ch from hook, (ch 3, skip next 3 chs, sc in next ch) across: 39 sc and 38 ch-3 sps.
Row 2: Ch 1, turn; sc in first sc, ★ ch 3, (sc, ch 5, sc) in next sc, ch 3, sc in next sc; repeat from ★ across: 57 sps.
Row 3: Ch 1, turn; sc in first sc and in next ch-3 sp, 7 dc in next ch-5 sp, ★ sc in next 2 ch-3 sps, 7 dc in next ch-5 sp; repeat from ★ across to last ch-3 sp, sc in last ch-3 sp and in last sc: 19 7-dc groups and 40 sc.

Row 4: Ch 4 **(counts as first tr)**, turn; skip next 2 sts, dc in next dc, ch 3, skip next dc, sc in next dc, ch 3, ★ decrease, ch 3, skip next dc, sc in next dc, ch 3; repeat from ★ across to last 5 sts, skip next dc, dc in next dc, skip next 2 sts, tr in last sc: 41 sts and 38 ch-3 sps.
Row 5: Ch 5 **(counts as first hdc plus ch 3)**, turn; skip next dc, hdc in next sc, ch 3, ★ hdc in next decrease, ch 3, hdc in next sc, ch 3; repeat from ★ across to last dc, skip last dc, hdc in last tr: 38 ch-3 sps.
Row 6: Ch 1, turn; sc in first hdc, (sc, work Picot, sc) in each ch-3 sp across to last hdc, sc in last hdc: 78 sc.
Row 7: Ch 6 **(counts as first dc plus ch 3, now and throughout)**, turn; skip next Picot and next sc, ★ dc in sp **before** next sc *(Fig. 20, page 141)*, ch 3, skip next Picot and next sc; repeat from ★ across to last sc, dc in last sc: 38 ch-3 sps.
Row 8: Ch 1, turn; sc in first dc, ★ ch 3, (sc, ch 5, sc) in next dc, ch 3, sc in next dc; repeat from ★ across: 57 sps.
Repeat Rows 3-8 until Afghan Body measures approximately 53¹/₂" from beginning ch, ending by working Row 4; do **not** finish off.

EDGING

Rnd 1: Ch 1, turn; sc in first tr, 2 sc in next ch-3 sp, 3 sc in each ch-3 sp across to last 2 sts, skip next dc, sc in last tr, place marker in sc just made to mark corner; work 167 sc evenly spaced across end of rows; working in free loops *(Fig. 17b, page 141)* and in sps across beginning ch, sc in first ch, place marker in sc just made to mark corner, 2 sc in next sp, 3 sc in each sp across to marked ch, sc in marked ch, remove marker and place in sc just made to mark corner; work 167 sc evenly spaced across end of rows; join with slip st to first sc: 564 sc.
Rnd 2: Ch 1, do **not** turn; 2 sc in same st, ★ sc in each sc across to next marked corner sc, 3 sc in marked corner sc, remove marker; repeat from ★ 2 times **more**, sc in each sc across and in same st as first sc; join with slip st to first sc: 572 sc.

Rnds 3 and 4: Ch 1, 2 sc in same st, ★ sc in each sc across to center sc of next corner 3-sc group, 3 sc in center sc; repeat from ★ 2 times **more**, sc in each sc across and in same st as first sc; join with slip st to first sc: 588 sc.

Rnd 5: Ch 6, ★ skip next 2 sc, (dc in next sc, ch 3, skip next 2 sc) across to center sc of next corner 3-sc group, (dc, ch 3) twice in center sc; repeat from ★ 2 times **more**, skip next 2 sc, (dc in next sc, ch 3, skip next 2 sc) across, dc in same st as first dc, ch 2, sc in first dc to form last ch-3 sp: 200 ch-3 sps.

Rnd 6: Ch 1, **turn**; (sc, work Picot, sc) in last ch-3 sp made, ★ (sc, work Picot, sc) in each ch-3 sp across to next corner ch-3 sp, [sc, (work Picot, sc) twice] in corner ch-3 sp, place marker in center sc of 3-sc group just made; repeat from ★ 2 times **more**, (sc, work Picot, sc) in each ch-3 sp across, sc in same sp as first sc, work Picot; join with slip st to first sc: 404 sc and 204 Picots.

Rnd 7: Ch 6, turn; ★ (skip next Picot and next sc, dc in sp **before** next sc, ch 3) across to next corner 3-sc group, (dc, ch 3) twice in marked corner sc, remove marker; repeat from ★ 2 times **more**, (skip next Picot and next sc, dc in sp **before** next sc, ch 3) across to last Picot, skip last Picot, dc in same st as first dc, ch 2, sc in first dc to form last ch-3 sp: 208 ch-3 sps.

Rnds 8-11: Repeat Rnds 6 and 7 twice: 224 dc.

Rnd 12: Ch 1, turn; sc in last ch-3 sp made, ch 3, ★ (sc, ch 5, sc) in next dc, ch 3, [sc in next dc, ch 3, (sc, ch 5, sc) in next dc, ch 3] across to next corner ch-3 sp, sc in corner ch-3 sp, ch 3; repeat from ★ 2 times **more**, (sc, ch 5, sc) in next dc, [ch 3, sc in next dc, ch 3, (sc, ch 5, sc) in next dc] across, ch 1, hdc in first sc to form last ch-3 sp: 342 sps.

Rnd 13: Ch 1, turn; sc in last ch-3 sp made, [dc, (work Picot, dc) 3 times] in next ch-5 sp, ★ sc in next 2 ch-3 sps, [dc, (work Picot, dc) 3 times] in next ch-5 sp; repeat from ★ around to last ch-3 sp, sc in last ch-3 sp; join with slip st to first sc, finish off.

Viola Patch

Springtime will stand still when you crochet this patchwork of blossoming violas. The floral wrap is made up of granny squares, and embroidery chain stitches form the flowers' delicate stems.

Finished Size: 60¹/₂" x 75¹/₂"

MATERIALS
Worsted Weight Yarn:
    White - 27¹/₂ ounces, (780 grams, 1,555 yards)
    Green - 23¹/₂ ounces, (670 grams, 1,330 yards)
    Lt Purple - 11¹/₂ ounces, (330 grams, 650 yards)
    Purple - 2¹/₂ ounces, (70 grams, 140 yards)
Crochet hook, size I (5.50 mm) **or** size needed for gauge
Yarn needle

GAUGE SWATCH: 3" square
Work same as Square A.

STITCH GUIDE

CHAIN STITCH
Chain stitch is worked from right to left. Make all stitches equal in length. Come up at 1 and make a counterclockwise loop with the yarn. Go down at 1 and come up at 2, keeping the yarn below the point of the needle *(Fig. 1a)*. Make a loop with the yarn and go down at 2; come up at 3, keeping yarn below the point of the needle *(Fig. 1b)*. Secure last loop by bringing yarn over loop and down.

Fig. 1a   **Fig. 1b**

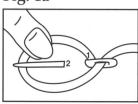
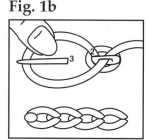

Continued on page 16.

SQUARE A

With color indicated, ch 4; join with slip st to form a ring.

Rnd 1 (Right side): Ch 3 **(counts as first dc, now and throughout)**, 2 dc in ring, (ch 2, 3 dc in ring) 3 times, hdc in first dc to form last ch-2 sp: 12 dc and 4 ch-2 sps.

Note: Loop a short piece of yarn around any stitch to mark Rnd 1 as **right** side.

Rnd 2: Ch 3, (2 dc, ch 2, 3 dc) in last ch-2 sp made, ch 1, ★ (3 dc, ch 2, 3 dc) in next ch-2 sp, ch 1; repeat from ★ 2 times **more**; join with slip st to first dc, finish off: 24 dc and 8 sps.

SQUARE B

With first color indicated, ch 4; join with slip st to form a ring.

Rnd 1 (Right side): Ch 5 **(counts as first dc plus ch 2)**, 3 dc in ring, cut first color, with second color indicated, YO and draw through, ch 1, (3 dc, ch 2, 3 dc) in ring, cut second color, with first color, YO and draw through, ch 1, 2 dc in ring; join with slip st to first dc: 12 dc and 4 ch-2 sps.

Note: Mark Rnd 1 as **right** side.

Rnd 2: Slip st in first ch-2 sp, ch 3, (2 dc, ch 2, 3 dc) in same sp, ch 1, 3 dc in next ch-2 sp, cut first color, with second color, YO and draw through, ch 1, 3 dc in same sp, ch 1, (3 dc, ch 2, 3 dc) in next ch-2 sp, ch 1, 3 dc in next ch-2 sp, cut second color, with first color, YO and draw through, ch 1, 3 dc in same sp, ch 1; join with slip st to first dc, finish off: 24 dc and 8 sps.

ASSEMBLY

With matching color, using Placement Diagram as a guide, and working through inside loops only, whipstitch Squares together *(Fig. 21a, page 142)*, forming 20 vertical strips of 25 Squares each; whipstitch strips together in same manner.

FINISHING

With Green and using Placement Diagram as a guide, work chain stitch for stems.

EDGING

With **right** side facing, join Green with sc in any corner ch-2 sp *(see Joining With Sc, page 140)*; ch 2, sc in same sp, (sc in next 3 dc and in next sp) twice, hdc in joining, (sc in next sp and in next 3 dc) twice, [sc in next sp, hdc in joining, (sc in next sp and in next 3 dc) twice] across to next corner ch-2 sp, ★ (sc, ch 2, sc) in corner ch-2 sp, (sc in next 3 dc and in next sp) twice, hdc in joining, (sc in next sp and in next 3 dc) twice, [sc in next sp, hdc in joining, (sc in next sp and in next 3 dc) twice] across to next corner ch-2 sp; repeat from ★ 2 times **more**; join with slip st to first sc, finish off.

PLACEMENT DIAGRAM

KEY
Square A
☐ - White (Make 188)
◻ - Lt Green (Make 156)
◼ - Lt Purple (Make 78)
Square B
◹ - White & Lt Green (Make 30)
◤ - White & Purple (Make 18)
◹ - White & Lt Purple (Make 12)
◩ - Purple & Lt Purple (Make 12)
◪ - Purple & Lt Green (Make 6)

Soft Clover

Irish eyes won't be the only ones smiling over this gorgeous afghan. Soft green yarn creates a look that resembles a majestic field of clover.

Finished Size: 48" x 68"

MATERIALS

Worsted Weight Yarn:
    52 ounces, (1,480 grams, 3,035 yards)
Crochet hook, size G (4.00 mm) **or** size needed for gauge

GAUGE: In pattern, 2 repeats and 10 rows = 4³/₄"

Gauge Swatch: 5"w x 4³/₄"h
Ch 24 **loosely**, place marker in last ch made for st placement, ch 3 **loosely**: 27 chs.
Work same as Afghan Body for 10 rows.
Finish off.

STITCH GUIDE

> **SHELL**
> 5 Dc in st indicated.

AFGHAN BODY

Ch 151 **loosely**, (place marker in last ch made for st placement, ch 3 **loosely**) twice: 157 chs.
Row 1 (Right side): Dc in 12th ch from hook, (ch 1, dc in same st) 3 times, ch 3, skip next 4 chs, tr in next ch, ★ ch 3, skip next 4 chs, dc in next ch, (ch 1, dc in same st) 3 times, ch 3, skip next 4 chs, tr in next ch; repeat from ★ across: 75 sps.
Row 2: Ch 1, turn; sc in first tr, ch 3, sc in next ch-1 sp, ch 3, (sc, ch 3) twice in next ch-1 sp, sc in next ch-1 sp, ch 3, ★ sc in next tr, ch 3, sc in next ch-1 sp, ch 3, (sc, ch 3) twice in next ch-1 sp, sc in next ch-1 sp, ch 3; repeat from ★ across, skip next dc, sc in first marked ch, remove marker.
Row 3: Ch 4 (counts as first dc plus ch 1), turn; (dc, ch 1, dc) in same st, ch 3, skip next 2 ch-3 sps, tr in next ch-3 sp, ch 3, ★ skip next 2 sc, dc in next sc, (ch 1, dc in same st) 3 times, ch 3, skip next 2 ch-3 sps, tr in next ch-3 sp, ch 3; repeat from ★ across to last 3 sc, skip next 2 sc, dc in last sc, (ch 1, dc in same st) twice: 76 sps.

Row 4: Ch 3, turn; sc in first ch-1 sp, ch 3, sc in next ch-1 sp, ch 3, sc in next tr, ch 3, sc in next ch-1 sp, ch 3, ★ (sc, ch 3) twice in next ch-1 sp, sc in next ch-1 sp, ch 3, skip next dc, sc in next tr, ch 3, sc in next ch-1 sp, ch 3; repeat from ★ across to last ch-1 sp, sc in last ch-1 sp, leave remaining dc unworked: 75 sps.
Row 5: Ch 7 (counts as first tr plus ch 3), turn; skip next sc, dc in next sc, (ch 1, dc in same st) 3 times, ch 3, skip next 2 ch-3 sps, tr in next ch-3 sp, ★ ch 3, skip next 2 sc, dc in next sc, (ch 1, dc in same st) 3 times, ch 3, skip next 2 ch-3 sps, tr in next ch-3 sp; repeat from ★ across.
Row 6: Ch 1, turn; sc in first tr, ★ ch 3, sc in next ch-1 sp, ch 3, (sc, ch 3) twice in next ch-1 sp, sc in next ch-1 sp, ch 3, sc in next tr; repeat from ★ across.
Rows 7-116: Repeat Rows 3-6, 27 times; then repeat Rows 3 and 4 once **more**; at end of Row 116, do **not** finish off.

EDGING

Rnd 1: Ch 1, turn; sc in first sc, ch 5, skip next sc, sc in next sc, ch 5, ★ skip next 2 ch-3 sps, sc in next ch-3 sp, ch 5, skip next 2 sc, sc in next sc, ch 5; repeat from ★ across to last 3 ch-3 sps, skip next 2 ch-3 sps, (sc, ch 5, sc) in last ch-3 sp, ch 4; working in end of rows, skip next row, (sc in next row, ch 4, skip next row) across; working in free loops of beginning ch *(Fig. 17b, page 141)*, (sc, ch 5) twice in first ch, skip next 4 chs, (sc in next ch, ch 5, skip next 4 chs) across to marked ch, (sc, ch 5, sc) in marked ch, ch 4; working in end of rows, skip first row, (sc in next row, ch 4, skip next row) across, sc in same st as first sc, ch 2, dc in first sc to form last corner ch-5 sp: 180 sc and 180 sps.
Rnd 2: Ch 1, sc in last ch-5 sp made, skip next sc, ★ † work Shell in next sc, (sc in next sp, ch 4, sc in next sp, work Shell in next sc) across to within one sp of next corner ch-5 sp, skip next sp †, (sc, ch 5, sc) in corner ch-5 sp, skip next sc; repeat from ★ 2 times **more**, then repeat from † to † once, sc in same sp as first sc, ch 2, dc in first sc to form last corner ch-5 sp: 88 Shells.

Continued on page 18.

Rnd 3: Ch 1, sc in last ch-5 sp made, ★ † work Shell in next sc, skip next 2 dc, sc in next dc, work Shell in next sc, (sc in next ch-4 sp, ch 4, skip next 3 sts, sc in next dc, ch 4, sc in next ch-4 sp, work Shell in next sc, skip next 2 dc, sc in next dc, work Shell in next sc) across to next corner ch-5 sp †, (sc, ch 5, sc) in corner ch-5 sp; repeat from ★ 2 times **more**, then repeat from † to † once, sc in same sp as first sc, ch 2, dc in first sc to form last corner ch-5 sp: 92 Shells.

Rnd 4: Ch 1, sc in last ch-5 sp made, ★ † work Shell in next sc, (skip next 2 dc, sc in next dc, work Shell in next sc) twice, [sc in next ch-4 sp, ch 4, sc in next ch-4 sp, work Shell in next sc, (skip next 2 dc, sc in next dc, work Shell in next sc) twice] across to next corner ch-5 sp †, (sc, ch 5, sc) in corner ch-5 sp; repeat from ★ 2 times **more**, then repeat from † to † once, sc in same sp as first sc, ch 2, dc in first sc to form last corner ch-5 sp: 138 Shells.

Rnd 5: Ch 1, sc in last ch-5 sp made, ★ † ch 4, skip next 3 sts, sc in next dc, (work Shell in next sc, skip next 2 dc, sc in next dc) twice, ch 4, [sc in next ch-4 sp, ch 4, skip next 3 sts, sc in next dc, (work Shell in next sc, skip next 2 dc, sc in next dc) twice, ch 4] across to next corner ch-5 sp †, (sc, ch 5, sc) in corner ch-5 sp; repeat from ★ 2 times **more**, then repeat from † to † once, sc in same sp as first sc, ch 2, dc in first sc to form last corner ch-5 sp: 92 Shells.

Rnd 6: Ch 1, sc in last ch-5 sp made, ★ † work Shell in next sc, (sc in next ch-4 sp, ch 4, skip next 3 sts, sc in next dc, work Shell in next sc, skip next 2 dc, sc in next dc, ch 4, sc in next ch-4 sp, work Shell in next sc) across to next corner ch-5 sp †, (sc, ch 5, sc) in corner ch-5 sp; repeat from ★ 2 times **more**, then repeat from † to † once, sc in same sp as first sc, ch 2, dc in first sc to form last corner ch-5 sp: 96 Shells.

Rnds 7 and 8: Repeat Rnds 3 and 4: 150 Shells.

Rnd 9: Ch 1, sc in last ch-5 sp made, ch 5, ★ † skip next 3 sts, sc in next dc, (work Shell in next sc, skip next 2 dc, sc in next dc) twice, [ch 4, sc in next ch-4 sp, ch 4, skip next 3 sts, sc in next dc, (work Shell in next sc, skip next 2 dc, sc in next dc) twice] across to next corner ch-5 sp, ch 5 †, sc in corner ch-5 sp, ch 5; repeat from ★ 2 times **more**, then repeat from † to † once; join with slip st to first sc: 100 Shells.

Rnd 10: Ch 3, 2 dc in same st, ★ † sc in next ch-5 sp, ch 4, skip next 3 sts, sc in next dc, work Shell in next sc, skip next 2 dc, sc in next dc, ch 4, sc in next ch-4 sp, (work Shell in next sc, sc in next ch-4 sp, ch 4, skip next 3 sts, sc in next dc, work Shell in next sc, skip next 2 dc, sc in next dc, ch 4, sc in next sp)

across to next corner sc †, 7 dc in corner sc; repeat from ★ 2 times **more**, then repeat from † to † once, 4 dc in same st as first dc; join with slip st to first dc: 96 Shells.

Rnd 11: Ch 1, sc in same st, ★ † ch 5, sc in next ch-4 sp, ch 4, skip next 3 sts, sc in next dc, ch 4, sc in next ch-4 sp, [work Shell in next sc, skip next 2 dc, sc in next dc, work Shell in next sc, sc in next ch-4 sp, ch 4, skip next 3 sts, sc in next dc, ch 4, sc in next ch-4 sp] across to next corner 7-dc group, ch 5, skip next 3 sts, sc in next dc †, ch 5, skip next dc, sc in next dc; repeat from ★ 2 times **more**, then repeat from † to † once, ch 2, dc in first sc to form last corner ch-5 sp: 92 Shells.

Rnd 12: Ch 1, sc in last ch-5 sp made, ★ † work Shell in next sc, sc in next ch-5 sp, (ch 4, sc in next ch-4 sp) twice, [work Shell in next sc, (skip next 2 dc, sc in next dc, work Shell in next sc) twice, sc in next ch-4 sp, ch 4, sc in next ch-4 sp] across to within one ch-5 sp of next corner ch-5 sp, ch 4, sc in next ch-5 sp, work Shell in next sc †, (sc, ch 5, sc) in corner ch-5 sp; repeat from ★ 2 times **more**, then repeat from † to † once, sc in same sp as first sc, ch 2, dc in first sc to form last corner ch-5 sp: 146 Shells.

Rnd 13: Ch 1, sc in last ch-5 sp made, ★ † ch 5, skip next 3 sts, sc in next dc, ch 5, sc in next ch-4 sp, ch 5, [sc in next ch-4 sp, ch 5, skip next 3 sts, sc in next dc, ch 5, (skip next 5 sts, sc in next dc, ch 5) twice, sc in next ch-4 sp, ch 5] across to within one ch-4 sp of next corner ch-5 sp, sc in next ch-4 sp, ch 5, skip next 3 sts, sc in next dc, ch 5 †, sc in corner ch-5 sp; repeat from ★ 2 times **more**, then repeat from † to † once; join with slip st to first sc: 208 ch-5 sps.

Rnd 14: Ch 3, 2 dc in same st, ★ † sc in next ch-5 sp, work Shell in next sc, sc in next ch-5 sp, (ch 5, sc in next ch-5 sp, work Shell in next sc, sc in next ch-5 sp) across to next corner sc †, 9 dc in corner sc; repeat from ★ 2 times **more**, then repeat from † to † once, 6 dc in same st as first dc; join with slip st to first dc: 104 Shells.

Rnd 15: Ch 1, sc in same st, ★ † ch 5, skip next 5 sts, (sc in next dc, ch 5, sc in next ch-5 sp, ch 5, skip next 3 sts) across to last Shell on same side, sc in next dc, ch 5, skip next 5 sts, sc in next dc †, ch 5, skip next 3 sts, sc in next dc; repeat from ★ 2 times **more**, then repeat from † to † once, ch 2, dc in first sc to form last corner ch-5 sp: 212 ch-5 sps.

Rnd 16: Ch 1, sc in last ch-5 sp made, ★ † work Shell in next sc, (sc in next ch-5 sp, ch 5, sc in next ch-5 sp, work Shell in next sc) across to next corner ch-5 sp †, (sc, ch 5, sc) in corner ch-5 sp; repeat from ★ 2 times **more**, then repeat from † to † once, sc in same sp as first sc, ch 5; join with slip st to first sc, finish off.

18

Floral Bounty

Abloom with exuberant flowers, this textured wrap is a delight!
An edging of plush cluster stitches adds the finishing touch.

Finished Size: 53" x 67"

MATERIALS
Worsted Weight Yarn:
53 ounces, (1,510 grams, 3,635 yards)
Crochet hook, size H (5.00 mm) **or** size needed for gauge
Yarn needle

GAUGE: Each Square = 7"

Gauge Swatch: $3^1/2$" diameter
Work same as Square through Rnd 2.

STITCH GUIDE

CLUSTER
Ch 3, YO, insert hook in third ch from hook, YO and pull up a loop, YO and draw through 2 loops on hook, YO, insert hook in same ch, YO and pull up a loop, YO and draw through 2 loops on hook, YO and draw through all 3 loops on hook *(Figs. 11a & b, page 139)*.

SQUARE (Make 63)

Rnd 1 (Right side): Ch 4, 15 dc in fourth ch from hook **(3 skipped chs count as first dc)**; join with slip st to first dc: 16 dc.
Note: Loop a short piece of yarn around any stitch to mark Rnd 1 as **right** side.
Rnd 2: Ch 5 **(counts as first tr plus ch 1)**, (tr in next dc, ch 1) around; join with slip st to first tr: 16 tr and 16 ch-1 sps.
Rnd 3: Ch 1, **turn**; sc in same st, work Cluster, (sc in next tr, work Cluster) around; join with slip st to first sc: 16 Clusters.
Rnd 4: Ch 1, turn; working **behind** Clusters *(Fig. 18, page 141)* and in ch-1 sps on Rnd 2, (sc in next ch-1 sp, ch 2) twice, (sc, ch 3, sc) in next ch-1 sp, ch 2, ★ (sc in next ch-1 sp, ch 2) 3 times, (sc, ch 3, sc) in next ch-1 sp, ch 2; repeat from ★ 2 times **more**, sc in last ch-1 sp, ch 2; join with slip st to first sc: 20 sps.

Rnd 5: Do **not** turn; slip st in first ch-2 sp, ch 1, sc in same sp, ch 1, skip next ch-2 sp, (tr, ch 1) 7 times in next ch-3 sp, skip next ch-2 sp, sc in next ch-2 sp, ★ ch 4, sc in next ch-2 sp, ch 1, skip next ch-2 sp, (tr, ch 1) 7 times in next ch-3 sp, skip next ch-2 sp, sc in next ch-2 sp; repeat from ★ 2 times **more**, ch 1, dc in first sc to form last ch-4 sp: 28 tr and 36 sps.
Rnd 6: Ch 1, sc in last ch-4 sp made, ★ † (ch 5, skip next ch-1 sp, sc in next ch-1 sp) twice, ch 7, (sc in next ch-1 sp, ch 5, skip next ch-1 sp) twice †, sc in next ch-4 sp; repeat from ★ 2 times **more**, then repeat from † to † once; join with slip st to first sc: 20 sps.
Rnd 7: Slip st in next 2 chs, ch 3 **(counts as first dc)**, 2 dc in same sp, ch 1, 3 dc in next ch-5 sp, ch 1, (3 dc, ch 3, 3 dc) in next corner ch-7 sp, ch 1, ★ (3 dc in next ch-5 sp, ch 1) 4 times, (3 dc, ch 3, 3 dc) in next corner ch-7 sp, ch 1; repeat from ★ 2 times **more**, (3 dc in next ch-5 sp, ch 1) twice; join with slip st to first dc, finish off: 72 dc and 24 sps.

ASSEMBLY

Working through both loops, whipstitch Squares together *(Fig. 21b, page 142)*, forming 7 vertical strips of 9 Squares each, beginning in center ch of first corner ch-3 and ending in center ch of next corner ch-3; whipstitch strips together in same manner.

EDGING

Rnd 1: With **right** side facing, join yarn with sc in any corner ch-3 sp *(see Joining With Sc, page 140)*; ch 3, sc in same sp, ★ † ch 1, skip next dc, sc in next dc, ch 1, (sc in next ch-1 sp, ch 1, skip next dc, sc in next dc, ch 1) 5 times, [(sc in next sp, ch 1) twice, skip next dc, sc in next dc, ch 1, (sc in next ch-1 sp, ch 1, skip next dc, sc in next dc, ch 1) 5 times] across to next corner ch-3 sp †, (sc, ch 3, sc) in corner ch-3 sp; repeat from ★ 2 times **more**, then repeat from † to † once; join with slip st to first sc: 416 sps.
Rnd 2: Slip st in first corner ch-3 sp, ch 1, (sc, ch 3, sc) in same sp, ch 1, (sc in next ch-1 sp, ch 1) across to next corner ch-3 sp, ★ (sc, ch 3, sc) in corner ch-3 sp, ch 1, (sc in next ch-1 sp, ch 1) across to next corner ch-3 sp; repeat from ★ 2 times **more**; join with slip st to first sc: 420 sps.

Continued on page 22.

Rnd 3: Slip st in first corner ch-3 sp, ch 1, **turn**; sc in same sp, work Cluster, ch 1, skip next ch-1 sp, (sc in next ch-1 sp, work Cluster, ch 1, skip next ch-1 sp) across to next corner ch-3 sp, ★ (sc, work Cluster, ch 1, sc) in corner ch-3 sp, work Cluster, ch 1, skip next ch-1 sp, (sc in next ch-1 sp, work Cluster, ch 1, skip next ch-1 sp) across to next corner ch-3 sp; repeat from ★ 2 times **more**, sc in same corner ch-3 sp as first sc, work Cluster, ch 1; join with slip st to first sc: 214 Clusters.

Rnd 4: Ch 1, turn; sc in same st, working **behind** next corner Cluster, (dc, ch 3, dc) in sp **before** next sc one rnd **below** corner Cluster, ★ sc in next sc, (ch 1, working **behind** next Cluster, dc in skipped ch-1 sp one rnd **below** Cluster, ch 1, sc in next sc) across to next corner Cluster, working **behind** corner Cluster, (dc, ch 3, dc) in sp **before** next sc one rnd **below** corner Cluster; repeat from ★ 2 times **more**, (sc in next sc, ch 1, working **behind** next Cluster, dc in skipped ch-1 sp one rnd **below** Cluster, ch 1) across; join with slip st to first sc: 432 sts and 424 sps.

Rnd 5: Slip st in next dc and in next corner ch-3 sp, ch 1, turn; sc in same sp, work Cluster, ch 1, (skip next sc, sc in next dc, work Cluster, ch 1) across to last sc on same side, skip last sc, ★ (sc, work Cluster, ch 1, sc) in corner ch-3 sp, work Cluster, ch 1, (skip next sc, sc in next dc, work Cluster, ch 1) across to last sc on same side, skip last sc; repeat from ★ 2 times **more**, sc in same corner ch-3 sp as first sc, work Cluster, ch 1; join with slip st to first sc: 218 Clusters.

Rnd 6: Ch 1, turn; sc in same st, working **behind** next corner Cluster, (dc, ch 3, dc) in sp **before** next sc one rnd **below** corner Cluster, ★ sc in next sc, (ch 1, working **behind** next Cluster, dc in skipped sc one rnd **below** Cluster, ch 1, sc in next sc) across to next corner Cluster, working **behind** corner Cluster, (dc, ch 3, dc) in sp **before** next sc one rnd **below** corner Cluster; repeat from ★ 2 times **more**, (sc in next sc, ch 1, working **behind** next Cluster, dc in skipped sc one rnd **below** Cluster, ch 1) across; join with slip st to first sc: 440 sts and 432 sps.

Rnds 7 and 8: Repeat Rnds 5 and 6: 448 sts and 440 sps.

Rnd 9: Do **not** turn; slip st in next dc, ch 1, slip st in next corner ch-3 sp, ch 1, slip st in next dc, ch 1, ★ (slip st in next ch-1 sp, ch 1) across to within 2 sts of next corner ch-3 sp, skip next sc, slip st in next dc, ch 1, slip st in corner ch-3 sp, ch 1, slip st in next dc, ch 1; repeat from ★ 2 times **more**, (slip st in next ch-1 sp, ch 1) across; join with slip st to first slip st, finish off.

Lullaby

As soft and soothing as a mother's lullaby, this coverlet of sport weight yarn will surround your little angel in handmade love.

Finished Size: 35" x 46"

MATERIALS
Sport Weight Yarn:
  14 ounces, (400 grams, 1,490 yards)
  Crochet hook, size G (4.00 mm) **or** size needed for gauge

GAUGE: In pattern, one repeat = $3^3/4$";
  5 rows = 3"

Gauge Swatch: $5^1/2$"w x $3^1/2$"h
Ch 37 **loosely**.
Work same as Afghan Body for 6 rows.
Finish off.

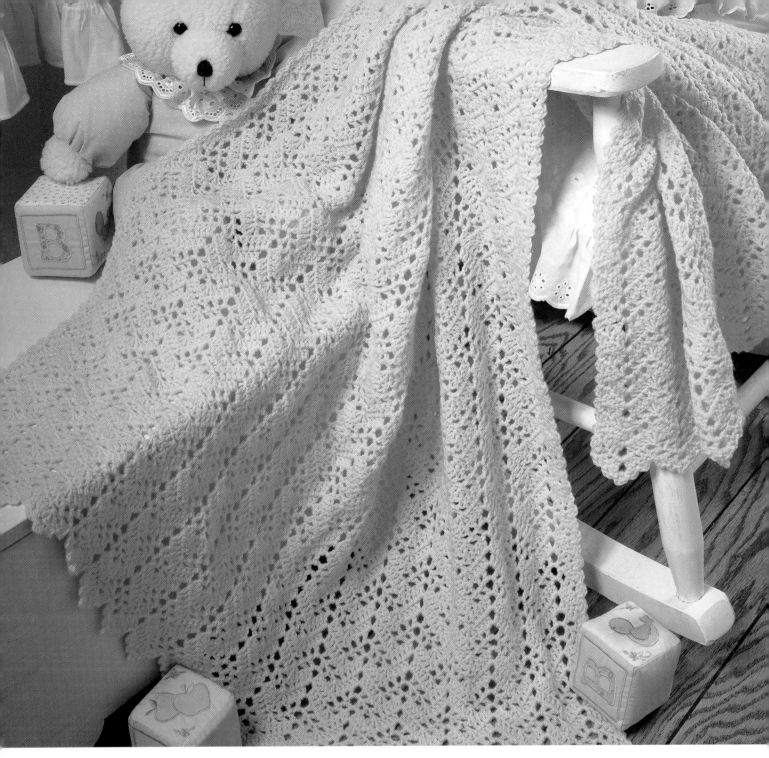

AFGHAN BODY

Ch 205 **loosely**.

Row 1 (Right side): Dc in fifth ch from hook and in next 2 chs, (dc, ch 3, dc) in next ch, ★ dc in next 3 chs, YO, insert hook in next ch, YO and pull up a loop, YO and draw through 2 loops on hook, (YO, skip **next** ch, insert hook in **next** ch, YO and pull up a loop, YO and draw through 2 loops on hook) twice, YO and draw through all 4 loops on hook, ch 1, skip next ch, dc in next ch, ch 1, skip next ch, (dc, ch 3, dc) in next ch, ch 1, skip next ch, dc in next ch, ch 1, (YO, skip **next** ch, insert hook in **next** ch, YO and pull up a loop, YO and draw through 2 loops on hook) 3 times, YO and draw through all 4 loops on hook, dc in next 3 chs, (dc, ch 3, dc) in next ch; repeat from ★ across to last 5 chs, dc in next 2 chs, YO, insert hook in next ch, YO and pull up a loop, YO and draw through 2 loops on hook, YO, skip next ch, insert hook in last ch, YO and pull up a loop, YO and draw through 2 loops on hook, YO and draw through all 3 loops on hook: 120 sts and 49 sps.

Continued on page 24.

Row 2: Ch 2, turn; skip first 2 sts, dc in next 2 dc, (2 dc, ch 3, 2 dc) in next ch-3 sp, ★ dc in next 2 dc, YO, insert hook in next dc, YO and pull up a loop, YO and draw through 2 loops on hook, YO, skip next ch-1 sp, insert hook in next dc, YO and pull up a loop, YO and draw through 2 loops on hook, YO and draw through all 3 loops on hook, ch 1, dc in next dc, ch 1, (dc, ch 3, dc) in next ch-3 sp, ch 1, dc in next dc, ch 1, YO, insert hook in next dc, YO and pull up a loop, YO and draw through 2 loops on hook, YO, skip next ch-1 sp and next 2 sts, insert hook in next dc, YO and pull up a loop, YO and draw through 2 loops on hook, YO and draw through all 3 loops on hook, dc in next 2 dc, (2 dc, ch 3, 2 dc) in next ch-3 sp; repeat from ★ across to last 4 dc, dc in next dc, YO, insert hook in next dc, YO and pull up a loop, YO and draw through 2 loops on hook, YO, skip next dc, insert hook in last dc, YO and pull up a loop, YO and draw through 2 loops on hook, YO and draw through all 3 loops on hook.

Row 3: Ch 2, turn; skip first 2 sts, dc in next 2 dc, ch 1, (dc, ch 3, dc) in next ch-3 sp, ch 1, dc in next dc, ★ ch 1, (YO, skip **next** dc, insert hook in **next** st, YO and pull up a loop, YO and draw through 2 loops on hook) twice, YO, insert hook in next dc, YO and pull up a loop, YO and draw through 2 loops on hook, YO and draw through all 4 loops on hook, dc in next ch-1 sp and in next dc, (2 dc, ch 3, 2 dc) in next ch-3 sp, dc in next dc and in next ch-1 sp, YO, insert hook in next dc, YO and pull up a loop, YO and draw through 2 loops on hook, YO, skip next ch-1 sp, insert hook in next st, YO and pull up a loop, YO and draw through 2 loops on hook, YO, skip next dc, insert hook in next dc, YO and pull up a loop, YO and draw through 2 loops on hook, YO and draw through all 4 loops on hook, ch 1, skip next dc, dc in next dc, ch 1, (dc, ch 3, dc) in next ch-3 sp, ch 1, dc in next dc; repeat from ★ across to last 3 dc, YO, insert hook in next dc, YO and pull up a loop, YO and draw through 2 loops on hook, YO, skip next dc, insert hook in last dc, YO and pull up a loop, YO and draw through 2 loops on hook, YO and draw through all 3 loops on hook: 118 sts and 51 sps.

Row 4: Ch 2, turn; dc in first ch-1 sp and in next dc, ch 1, (dc, ch 3, dc) in next ch-3 sp, ch 1, dc in next dc, ★ ch 1, YO, insert hook in next dc, YO and pull up a loop, YO and draw through 2 loops on hook, YO, skip next ch-1 sp and next 2 sts, insert hook in next dc, YO and pull up a loop, YO and draw through 2 loops on hook, YO and draw through all 3 loops on hook, dc in next 2 dc, (2 dc, ch 3, 2 dc) in next ch-3 sp, dc in next 2 dc, YO, insert hook in next dc,

YO and pull up a loop, YO and draw through 2 loops on hook, YO, skip next ch-1 sp, insert hook in next dc, YO and pull up a loop, YO and draw through 2 loops on hook, YO and draw through all 3 loops on hook, ch 1, dc in next dc, ch 1, (dc, ch 3, dc) in next ch-3 sp, ch 1, dc in next dc; repeat from ★ across to last ch-1 sp, YO, insert hook in last ch-1 sp, YO and pull up a loop, YO and draw through 2 loops on hook, YO, skip next dc, insert hook in last dc, YO and pull up a loop, YO and draw through 2 loops on hook, YO and draw through all 3 loops on hook.

Row 5: Ch 2, turn; dc in first ch-1 sp and in next dc, (2 dc, ch 3, 2 dc) in next ch-3 sp, ★ dc in next dc and in next ch-1 sp, YO, insert hook in next dc, YO and pull up a loop, YO and draw through 2 loops on hook, YO, skip next ch-1 sp, insert hook in next st, YO and pull up a loop, YO and draw through 2 loops on hook, YO, skip next dc, insert hook in next dc, YO and pull up a loop, YO and draw through 2 loops on hook, YO and draw through all 4 loops on hook, ch 1, skip next dc, dc in next dc, ch 1, (dc, ch 3, dc) in next ch-3 sp, ch 1, dc in next dc, ch 1, (YO, skip **next** dc, insert hook in **next** st, YO and pull up a loop, YO and draw through 2 loops on hook) twice, YO, insert hook in next dc, YO and pull up a loop, YO and draw through 2 loops on hook, YO and draw through all 4 loops on hook, dc in next ch-1 sp and in next dc, (2 dc, ch 3, 2 dc) in next ch-3 sp; repeat from ★ across to last 3 dc, dc in next dc, YO, insert hook in next ch-1 sp, YO and pull up a loop, YO and draw through 2 loops on hook, YO, skip next dc, insert hook in last dc, YO and pull up a loop, YO and draw through 2 loops on hook, YO and draw through all 3 loops on hook: 120 sts and 49 sps.

Repeat Rows 2-5 until Afghan measures approximately 45" from beginning ch, ending by working Row 2; do **not** finish off.

EDGING

Turn; (slip st, ch 2, hdc) in first st, skip next dc, (slip st, ch 2, hdc) in next dc, (slip st, ch 2, hdc, ch 1, slip st, ch 2, hdc) in next ch-3 sp, skip next dc, (slip st, ch 2, hdc) in next dc, skip next dc, ★ slip st in next 2 sts, (slip st, ch 2, hdc) in next ch, skip next dc, (slip st, ch 2, hdc) in next ch, (slip st, ch 2, hdc, ch 1, slip st, ch 2, hdc) in next ch-3 sp, skip next dc, (slip st, ch 2, hdc) in next ch, skip next dc, slip st in next ch and in next st, (slip st, ch 2, hdc) in next dc, skip next dc, (slip st, ch 2, hdc) in next dc, (slip st, ch 2, hdc, ch 1, slip st, ch 2, hdc) in next ch-3 sp, skip next dc, (slip st, ch 2, hdc) in next dc, skip next dc; repeat from ★ 7 times **more**, (slip st, ch 2, dc) in last dc; working in end of rows, skip first row, (slip st, ch 2, dc) in top of next row and each row across; working in free loops of beginning ch *(Fig. 17b, page 141)*, (slip st, ch 2, hdc, ch 1, slip st, ch 2, hdc) in first ch, skip next ch, (slip st, ch 2, hdc) in next ch, skip next ch, slip st in next 2 chs, † (slip st, ch 2, hdc) in next ch, skip next ch, (slip st, ch 2, hdc) in next ch, skip next 2 chs, (slip st, ch 2, hdc, ch 1, slip st, ch 2, hdc) in next ch, skip next 2 chs, (slip st, ch 2, hdc) in next ch, skip next ch, slip st in next 2 chs †; repeat from † to † 15 times **more**, [(slip st, ch 2, hdc) in next ch, skip next ch] twice, (slip st, ch 2, hdc, ch 1, slip st, ch 2, dc) in next ch; working in end of rows, (slip st, ch 2, dc) in top of each row across to last row, skip last row; join with slip st to st at base of beginning ch-2, finish off.

Enchantment

You'll be enchanted by this two-tone throw's delightful diamonds, created while working with only one color at a time. Cluster stitches produce the touch-tempting texture.

Finished Size: 48" x 65"

MATERIALS
Worsted Weight Yarn:
Purple - 31$\frac{1}{2}$ ounces, (890 grams, 2,160 yards)
Lt Purple - 27 ounces, (770 grams, 1,850 yards)
Crochet hook, size I (5.50 mm) **or** size needed for gauge

GAUGE: In pattern, (sc, ch 1) 7 times = 3$\frac{3}{4}$";
14 rows = 4"

Gauge Swatch: 4" square
Ch 16.
Row 1: Sc in second ch from hook, ★ ch 1, skip next ch, sc in next ch; repeat from ★ across: 8 sc.
Rows 2-14: Ch 1, turn; sc in first sc, (ch 1, sc in next sc) across.
Finish off.

STITCH GUIDE

CLUSTER
Ch 3, YO, insert hook in third ch from hook, YO and pull up a loop, YO and draw through 2 loops on hook, YO, insert hook in same ch, YO and pull up a loop, YO and draw through 2 loops on hook, YO and draw through all 3 loops on hook *(Figs. 11a & b, page 139)*.

Note: Each row is worked across length of Afghan. When joining yarn and finishing off, leave an 8" length to be worked into fringe.

AFGHAN BODY
With Lt Purple, ch 242.
Row 1 (Right side): Sc in second ch from hook, ★ ch 1, skip next ch, sc in next ch; repeat from ★ across; finish off: 121 sc and 120 ch-1 sps.
*Note: Loop a short piece of yarn around any stitch to mark Row 1 as **right** side.*
Row 2: With **wrong** side facing, join Purple with sc in first sc *(see Joining With Sc, page 140)*; ch 1, sc in next sc) 7 times, (work Cluster, skip next sc and next ch-1 sp, sc in next st 4 times, ★ (ch 1, sc in next sc) 6 times, (work Cluster, skip next sc and next ch-1 sp, sc in next st) 4 times; repeat from ★ across to last 7 sc, (ch 1, sc in next sc) 7 times; finish off: 89 sc and 32 Clusters.
Row 3: With **right** side facing, join Lt Purple with sc in first sc; (ch 1, sc in next sc) 7 times, [ch 1, working **behind** next Cluster *(Fig. 18, page 141)*, dc in skipped sc one row **below** Cluster, ch 1, sc in next sc] 4 times, ★ (ch 1, sc in next sc) 6 times, (ch 1, working **behind** next Cluster, dc in skipped sc one row **below** Cluster, ch 1, sc in next sc) 4 times; repeat from ★ across to last 7 sc, (ch 1, sc in next sc) 7 times; finish off: 121 sts and 120 ch-1 sps.
Row 4: With **wrong** side facing, join Purple with sc in first sc; (ch 1, skip next ch-1 sp, sc in next st) 8 times, ★ (work Cluster, skip next sc and next ch-1 sp, sc in next st) 3 times, (ch 1, skip next ch-1 sp, sc in next st) 8 times; repeat from ★ across; finish off: 97 sc and 24 Clusters.

Continued on page 26.

Row 5: With **right** side facing, join Lt Purple with sc in first sc; (ch 1, sc in next sc) 8 times, ★ (ch 1, working **behind** next Cluster, dc in skipped sc one row **below** Cluster, ch 1, sc in next sc) 3 times, (ch 1, sc in next sc) 8 times; repeat from ★ across; finish off: 121 sts and 120 ch-1 sps.

Row 6: With **wrong** side facing, join Purple with sc in first sc; (ch 1, skip next ch-1 sp, sc in next st) 3 times, work Cluster, skip next sc and next ch-1 sp, sc in next st, ★ (ch 1, skip next ch-1 sp, sc in next st) 4 times, (work Cluster, skip next sc and next ch-1 sp, sc in next st) twice, (ch 1, skip next ch-1 sp, sc in next st) 4 times, work Cluster, skip next sc and next ch-1 sp, sc in next st; repeat from ★ across to last 3 sc, (ch 1, sc in next sc) 3 times; finish off: 96 sc and 25 Clusters.

Row 7: With **right** side facing, join Lt Purple with sc in first sc; ch 1, (sc in next sc, ch 1) 3 times, working **behind** next Cluster, dc in skipped sc one row **below** Cluster, ★ ch 1, (sc in next sc, ch 1) 5 times, (working **behind** next Cluster, dc in skipped sc one row **below** Cluster, ch 1, sc in next sc, ch 1) twice, (sc in next sc, ch 1) 4 times, working **behind** next Cluster, dc in skipped sc one row **below** Cluster; repeat from ★ across to last 4 sc, (ch 1, sc in next sc) 4 times; finish off: 121 sts and 120 ch-1 sps.

Row 8: With **wrong** side facing, join Purple with sc in first sc; (ch 1, skip next ch-1 sp, sc in next st) twice, (work Cluster, skip next sc and next ch-1 sp, sc in next st) twice, ★ (ch 1, skip next ch-1 sp, sc in next st) 4 times, work Cluster, skip next sc and next ch-1 sp, sc in next st, (ch 1, skip next ch-1 sp, sc in next st) 4 times, (work Cluster, skip next sc and next ch-1 sp, sc in next st) twice; repeat from ★ across to last 2 sc, (ch 1, sc in next sc) twice; finish off: 95 sc and 26 Clusters.

Row 9: With **right** side facing, join Lt Purple with sc in first sc; (ch 1, sc in next sc) twice, (ch 1, working **behind** next Cluster, dc in skipped sc one row **below** Cluster, ch 1, sc in next sc) twice, ★ ch 1, (sc in next sc, ch 1) 4 times, working **behind** next Cluster, dc in skipped sc one row **below** Cluster, (ch 1, sc in next sc) 5 times, (ch 1, working **behind** next Cluster, dc in skipped sc one row **below** Cluster, ch 1, sc in next sc) twice; repeat from ★ across to last 2 sc, (ch 1, sc in next sc) twice; finish off: 121 sts and 120 ch-1 sps.

Row 10: With **wrong** side facing, join Purple with sc in first sc; ch 1, skip next ch-1 sp, sc in next st, (work Cluster, skip next sc and next ch-1 sp, sc in next st) 3 times, ★ (ch 1, skip next ch-1 sp, sc in next st) 8 times, (work Cluster, skip next sc and next ch-1 sp, sc in next st) 3 times; repeat from ★ across to last sc, ch 1, sc in last sc; finish off: 94 sc and 27 Clusters.

Row 11: With **right** side facing, join Lt Purple with sc in first sc; ch 1, sc in next sc, ch 1, (working **behind** next Cluster, dc in skipped sc one row **below** Cluster, ch 1, sc in next sc, ch 1) 3 times, ★ (sc in next sc, ch 1) 8 times, (working **behind** next Cluster, dc in skipped sc one row **below** Cluster, ch 1, sc in next sc, ch 1) 3 times; repeat from ★ across to last sc, sc in last sc; finish off: 121 sts and 120 ch-1 sps.

Row 12: With **wrong** side facing, join Purple with sc in first sc; (work Cluster, skip next sc and next ch-1 sp, sc in next st) 4 times, ★ (ch 1, sc in next sc) 6 times, (work Cluster, skip next sc and next ch-1 sp, sc in next st) 4 times; repeat from ★ across; finish off: 85 sc and 36 Clusters.

Row 13: With **right** side facing, join Lt Purple with sc in first sc; (ch 1, working **behind** next Cluster, dc in skipped sc one row **below** Cluster, ch 1, sc in next sc) 4 times, ★ (ch 1, sc in next sc) 6 times, (ch 1, working **behind** next Cluster, dc in skipped sc one row **below** Cluster, ch 1, sc in next sc) 4 times; repeat from ★ across; finish off: 121 sts and 120 ch-1 sps.

Rows 14 and 15: Repeat Rows 10 and 11.
Rows 16 and 17: Repeat Rows 8 and 9.
Rows 18 and 19: Repeat Rows 6 and 7.
Rows 20 and 21: Repeat Rows 4 and 5.
Rows 22-163: Repeat Rows 2-21, 7 times; then repeat Rows 2 and 3 once **more**; at end of Row 163, do **not** finish off.

TRIM
FIRST SIDE
Row 1: Ch 1, turn; sc in first sc, ★ ch 1, skip next ch-1 sp, sc in next st; repeat from ★ across: 121 sc and 120 ch-1 sps.
Row 2: Turn; slip st in first sc, (slip st in next ch-1 sp, ch 1) across to last ch-1 sp, slip st in last ch-1 sp and in last sc; finish off.

SECOND SIDE
With **right** side facing and working across beginning ch, join Lt Purple with slip st in free loop of first ch *(Fig. 17b, page 141)*; slip st in next sp, (ch 1, slip st in next sp) across to ch at base of last sc, slip st in ch at base of last sc; finish off.

Holding 3 strands of Lt Purple **and** 3 strands of Purple yarn together, each 17" long, add additional fringe in every other row across short edges of Afghan *(Figs. 22b & d, page 142)*.

Veranda

This wrap is ideal for cool spring evenings spent on the veranda watching the sun set. The design is worked in strips and then whipstitched together.

Finished Size: 47" x 63¹/₂"

MATERIALS
Worsted Weight Yarn:
   Ecru - 33 ounces, (940 grams, 2,265 yards)
   Blue - 7¹/₂ ounces, (210 grams, 515 yards)
Crochet hook, size J (6.00 mm) **or** size needed for
   gauge
Yarn needle

GAUGE: Each Strip = 6³/₄" wide

Gauge Swatch: 4"w x 3¹/₂"h
Work same as Center through Row 5.

STITCH GUIDE

> **FRONT POST TREBLE CROCHET**
>   *(abbreviated FPtr)*
> YO twice, insert hook from **front** to **back** around
> post of st indicated *(Fig. 10, page 139)*, YO and
> pull up a loop (4 loops on hook), (YO and draw
> through 2 loops on hook) 3 times. Skip st behind
> FPtr.

STRIP (Make 7)
CENTER
With Ecru, ch 17 **loosely**.
Row 1 (Right side): Dc in fourth ch from hook
(3 skipped chs count as first dc) and in each ch
across: 15 dc.
Note: Loop a short piece of yarn around any stitch
to mark Row 1 as **right** side and bottom edge.
Row 2: Ch 3 **(counts as first dc, now and
throughout)**, turn; ★ dc in next dc, skip next 2 dc,
5 dc in next dc, skip next 2 dc; repeat from ★ once
more, dc in last 2 dc.
Rows 3-84: Ch 3, turn; ★ dc in next dc, skip next
2 dc, 5 dc in next dc, skip next 2 dc; repeat from ★
once **more**, dc in last 2 dc.
Row 85: Ch 3, turn; dc in next dc and in each dc
across; finish off.

BORDER
Rnd 1: With **right** side facing and working in end of
rows, join Blue with slip st in Row 1; ch 3, 2 dc in
same row, (2 dc in next row, 3 dc in next row) across;
working in sts on Row 85, skip first 3 dc, 5 dc in
next dc, skip next 3 dc, 7 tr in next dc, skip next 3 dc,
5 dc in next dc, skip last 3 dc; working in end of
rows, 3 dc in first row, (2 dc in next row, 3 dc in next
row) across; working in free loops of beginning ch
(Fig. 17b, page 141), skip first 3 chs, 5 dc in next ch,
skip next 3 chs, 7 tr in next ch, skip next 3 chs, 5 dc
in next ch, skip last 3 chs; join with slip st to first dc,
finish off: 460 sts.
Rnd 2: With **right** side facing, skip first dc and join
Ecru with slip st in next dc; ch 3, 2 dc in same st,
skip next dc, † ★ work FPtr around each of next
2 dc, skip next dc, 3 dc in next dc, skip next dc;
repeat from ★ across to next 5-dc group, work FPtr
around each of next 2 dc, 3 dc in next dc, work FPtr
around each of next 2 dc, skip next tr, 3 dc in next tr,
work 2 FPtr around each of next 3 tr, 3 dc in next tr,
skip next tr, work FPtr around each of next 2 dc, 3 dc
in next dc, work FPtr around each of next 2 dc, skip
next dc †, 3 dc in next dc, skip next dc, repeat from
† to † once; join with slip st to first dc: 478 sts.
Rnd 3: Ch 1, working in Back Loops Only *(Fig. 16,
page 141)*, sc in same st and in next 2 dc, place
marker around last sc made for joining placement,
sc in next 208 sts, place marker around last sc made
for joining placement, sc in next 31 sts, place marker
around last sc made for joining placement, sc in next
208 sts, place marker around last sc made for joining
placement, sc in last 28 sts; join with slip st to **both**
loops of first sc, finish off.

ASSEMBLY
With Ecru and working through inside loops only,
whipstitch long edge of Strips together *(Fig. 21a,
page 142)*, beginning in first marked sc and ending
in next marked sc.

Blushing Beauty

As pretty as a blushing bride, this endearing wrap is covered in dainty little bows. A picot edging adds the complementary finale.

Finished Size: 46" x 64"

MATERIALS
Worsted Weight Yarn:
47 ounces, (1,330 grams, 3,225 yards)
Crochet hook, size I (5.50 mm) **or** size needed for gauge

GAUGE: In pattern, 14 sts = 4"; 8 rows = $3^1/_4$"

Gauge Swatch: $3^1/_4$" square
Ch 13 **loosely**.
Work same as Afghan Body for 8 rows.
Finish off.

STITCH GUIDE

BOW
Insert hook through **both** loops of next sc, † YO and pull up a loop, (YO and draw through one loop on hook) 6 times to form a ch †, working **behind** ch just made, insert hook in same st, YO and pull up a loop, (YO and draw through one loop on hook) 4 times to form a ch, working **behind** ch just made, insert hook in same st, repeat from † to † once, YO and draw through all 4 loops on hook.

PICOT
Ch 4, slip st in top of sc just made (**Fig. 1, page 56**).

AFGHAN BODY

Ch 157 **loosely**, place marker in third ch from hook for Edging placement.
Row 1 (Right side): Dc in fourth ch from hook and in each ch across (**3 skipped chs count as first dc**): 155 dc.
Row 2: Ch 1, turn; sc in BLO of first dc (**Fig. 16, page 141**), sc in FLO of next dc, (sc in BLO of next dc, sc in FLO of next dc) across to last dc, sc in last dc.
Row 3: Ch 3 (**counts as first dc, now and throughout**), turn; (dc in FLO of next sc, dc in BLO of next sc) across.
Row 4: Ch 1, turn; sc in BLO of first dc, sc in FLO of next dc, (sc in BLO of next dc, sc in FLO of next dc) across to last dc, sc in last dc.

Row 5: Ch 1, turn; pull up a loop in BLO of first sc and in FLO of next sc, YO and draw through all 3 loops on hook (**counts as one sc**), sc in BLO of next sc, sc in FLO of next sc, sc in **both** loops of next sc, work Bow, sc in **both** loops of next sc, sc in FLO of next sc, ★ (sc in BLO of next sc, sc in FLO of next sc) 4 times, sc in **both** loops of next sc, work Bow, sc in **both** loops of next sc, sc in FLO of next sc; repeat from ★ across to last 3 sc, sc in BLO of next sc, sc in FLO of next sc, 2 sc in BLO of last sc: 13 Bows and 142 sc.
Row 6: Ch 1, turn; sc in FLO of first sc, sc in BLO of next sc, (sc in FLO of next sc, sc in BLO of next sc) twice, sc in **both** loops of next Bow, ★ sc in BLO of next sc, (sc in FLO of next sc, sc in BLO of next sc) 5 times, sc in **both** loops of next Bow; repeat from ★ across to last 4 sc, (sc in BLO of next sc, sc in FLO of next sc) twice: 155 sc.
Row 7: Ch 3, turn; (dc in BLO of next sc, dc in FLO of next sc) across.
Row 8: Ch 1, turn; sc in FLO of first dc, sc in BLO of next dc, (sc in FLO of next dc, sc in BLO of next dc) across to last dc, sc in last dc.
Rows 9-12: Repeat Rows 7 and 8 twice.
Row 13: Ch 1, turn; pull up a loop in FLO of first sc and in BLO of next sc, YO and draw through all 3 loops on hook (**counts as one sc**), (sc in FLO of next sc, sc in BLO of next sc) 4 times, ★ sc in **both** loops of next sc, work Bow, sc in **both** loops of next sc, sc in BLO of next sc, (sc in FLO of next sc, sc in BLO of next sc) 4 times; repeat from ★ across to last sc, 2 sc in FLO of last sc: 12 Bows and 143 sc.
Row 14: Ch 1, turn; sc in BLO of first sc, ★ sc in FLO of next sc, (sc in BLO of next sc, sc in FLO of next sc) 5 times, sc in **both** loops of next Bow; repeat from ★ across to last 10 sc, (sc in FLO of next sc, sc in BLO of next sc) 5 times: 155 sc.
Row 15: Ch 3, turn; (dc in FLO of next sc, dc in BLO of next sc) across.
Row 16: Ch 1, turn; sc in BLO of first dc, sc in FLO of next dc, (sc in BLO of next dc, sc in FLO of next dc) across to last dc, sc in last dc.
Rows 17-20: Repeat Rows 15 and 16 twice.
Rows 21-153: Repeat Rows 5-20, 8 times; then repeat Rows 5-9 once **more**; do **not** finish off.

Continued on page 32.

EDGING

Rnd 1: Ch 1, do **not** turn; sc in top of last dc made; work 190 sc evenly spaced across end of rows; working in free loops of beginning ch *(Fig. 17b, page 141)*, 3 sc in first ch, work 154 sc evenly spaced across to marked ch, 3 sc in marked ch; work 190 sc evenly spaced across end of rows; working in sts across Row 153, 3 sc in first dc, work 154 sc evenly spaced across, 2 sc in same st as first sc; join with slip st to first sc: 700 sc.

Rnd 2: Ch 1, sc in same st and in next sc, ★ † work Picot, (sc in next 4 sc, work Picot) across to within one sc of next corner 3-sc group, sc in next 2 sc, ch 3, skip next sc †, sc in next 2 sc; repeat from ★ 2 times **more**, then repeat from † to † once; join with slip st to first sc, finish off.

Reverie

Spend the afternoon daydreaming while snuggled in the comfort of this plush throw. Long single crochets make up the mesmerizing pattern, and fringe adds the finishing touch.

Finished Size: 48$\frac{1}{2}$" x 68"

MATERIALS
Worsted Weight Yarn:
Blue - 30 ounces, (850 grams, 2,055 yards)
Ecru - 28 ounces, (800 grams, 1,920 yards)
Crochet hook, size H (5.00 mm) **or** size needed for gauge

GAUGE: In pattern, (5 sts, ch 3) twice = 3$\frac{1}{2}$"; 12 rows = 2$\frac{3}{4}$"

Gauge Swatch: 4$\frac{1}{2}$"w x 3$\frac{1}{4}$"h
Ch 22 **loosely**.
Work same as Afghan for 14 rows.

STITCH GUIDE

LONG SINGLE CROCHET
(abbreviated LSC)
Working **around** previous row, insert hook in ch-3 sp one row **below** next ch, YO and pull up a loop even with last sc made, YO and draw through both loops on hook *(Fig. 9, page 139)*.

AFGHAN

With Blue, ch 222 **loosely**.
Row 1 (Right side): Sc in second ch from hook, ★ ch 3, skip next 3 chs, sc in next 5 chs; repeat from ★ across to last 4 chs, ch 3, skip next 3 chs, sc in last ch: 137 sc and 28 ch-3 sps.
Note: Loop a short piece of yarn around any stitch to mark Row 1 as **right** side.

Row 2: Ch 1, turn; sc in first sc, ch 3, (sc in next 5 sc, ch 3) across to last sc, sc in last sc; finish off.
Row 3: With **right** side facing, join Ecru with sc in first sc *(see Joining With Sc, page 140)*; working in Back Loops Only *(Fig. 16, page 141)*, sc in next ch, work LSC, ★ sc in next ch and in next sc, ch 3, skip next 3 sc, sc in next sc and in next ch, work LSC; repeat from ★ across to last ch, sc in last ch and in **both** loops of last sc; do **not** finish off: 140 sts and 27 ch-3 sps.
Row 4: Ch 1, turn; working in both loops, sc in first 5 sts, ★ ch 3, skip next ch-3 sp, sc in next 5 sts; repeat from ★ across; finish off.
Row 5: With **right** side facing, join Blue with sc in first sc; ★ ch 3, skip next 3 sc, working in Back Loops Only, sc in next sc and in next ch, work LSC, sc in next ch and in next sc; repeat from ★ across to last 4 sc, ch 3, skip next 3 sc, sc in **both** loops of last sc; do **not** finish off: 137 sts and 28 ch-3 sps.
Row 6: Ch 1, turn; working in both loops, sc in first sc, ★ ch 3, skip next ch-3 sp, sc in next 5 sts; repeat from ★ across to last ch-3 sp, ch 3, skip last ch-3 sp, sc in last sc; finish off.
Repeat Rows 3-6 until Afghan measures approximately 68" from beginning ch, ending by working Row 6.

Holding 7 strands of Blue yarn together, each 22" long, add fringe in spaces across short edges of Afghan *(Figs. 22a & c, page 142)*.

Picturesque Posies

Everyone will admire your blossoming crochet talents when you cultivate this rosy posy cover-up.
The design features sport weight flowers surrounded by worsted weight squares.

Finished Size: 52¹/₂" x 65"

MATERIALS
Worsted Weight Yarn:
 Aran - 40 ounces, (1,140 grams, 2,260 yards)
 Rose - 3¹/₂ ounces, (100 grams, 200 yards)
Sport Weight Yarn:
 Rose - 15 ounces, (430 grams, 1,500 yards)
Crochet hooks, sizes E (3.50 mm) **and**
 H (5.00 mm) **or** sizes needed for gauge
Yarn needle

GAUGE: Rnds 1-3 of Posy = 2";
 Each Square = 7¹/₂ "

STITCH GUIDE

DC DECREASE
YO, insert hook in **same** sp, YO and pull up a loop, YO and draw through 2 loops on hook, YO, skip next 2 joined sps, insert hook in **next** ch-5 sp, YO and pull up a loop, YO and draw through 2 loops on hook, YO and draw through all 3 loops on hook **(counts as one dc)**.

SC DECREASE
Pull up a loop in next 2 sts, YO and draw through all 3 loops on hook **(counts as one sc)**.

PUFF ST
★ YO, insert hook in st indicated, YO and pull up a loop even with last st made; repeat from ★ 2 times **more**, YO and draw through all 7 loops on hook *(Fig. 13, page 139)*.

SQUARE (Make 36)
POSY CLUSTER
FIRST POSY
Rnd 1 (Right side): With Sport Weight Rose and smaller size hook, ch 2, 4 sc in second ch from hook; join with slip st to first sc.
Note: Loop a short piece of yarn around any stitch to mark Rnd 1 as **right** side.
Rnd 2: Ch 1, (sc, ch 3) twice in same st and in each sc around; join with slip st to first sc: 8 ch-3 sps.

Rnd 3: Slip st in first ch-3 sp, ch 1, (sc, hdc, dc, hdc, sc) in same sp and in each ch-3 sp around; do **not** join: 8 Petals.
Rnd 4: Working **behind** Petals, slip st in leg at back of first sc on first Petal, ch 5, (slip st in leg at back of first sc on next Petal, ch 5) around; working **below** first slip st, join with slip st to same leg as first slip st, place marker around last ch-5 made for st placement, finish off: 8 ch-5 sps.

SECOND POSY
Work same as First Posy through Rnd 3: 8 Petals.
Rnd 4 (Joining rnd): Working **behind** Petals, slip st in leg at back of first sc on first Petal, (ch 5, slip st in leg at back of first sc on next Petal) twice, place marker around last ch-5 made for st placement, (ch 5, slip st in leg at back of first sc on next Petal) 4 times, ch 2; holding Posies with **wrong** sides together, slip st in marked ch-5 sp on **First Posy**, remove marker, ch 2, slip st in leg at back of first sc on next Petal on **Second Posy**, ch 2, slip st in next ch-5 sp on **First Posy**, ch 2; working **below** first slip st on **Second Posy**, join with slip st to same leg as first slip st, finish off.

THIRD POSY
Work same as First Posy through Rnd 3: 8 Petals.
Rnd 4 (Joining rnd): Working **behind** Petals, slip st in leg at back of first sc on first Petal, (ch 5, slip st in leg at back of first sc on next Petal) twice, place marker around last ch-5 made for st placement, (ch 5, slip st in leg at back of first sc on next Petal) 4 times, ch 2; holding Posies with **wrong** sides together, slip st in marked ch-5 sp on **Second Posy**, remove marker, ch 2, slip st in leg at back of first sc on next Petal on **Third Posy**, ch 2, slip st in next ch-5 sp on **Second Posy**, ch 2; working **below** first slip st on **Third Posy**, join with slip st to same leg as first slip st, finish off.

FOURTH POSY
Work same as First Posy through Rnd 3: 8 Petals.

Continued on page 36.

Rnd 4 (Joining rnd): Working **behind** Petals, slip st in leg at back of first sc on first Petal, (ch 5, slip st in leg at back of first sc on next Petal) twice, place marker around last ch-5 made for st placement, (ch 5, slip st in leg at back of first sc on next Petal) twice, ch 2; holding Posies with **wrong** sides together, slip st in marked ch-5 sp on **Third Posy**, remove marker, ch 2, slip st in leg at back of first sc on next Petal on **Fourth Posy**, ch 2, slip st in next ch-5 sp on **Third Posy**, ch 2, slip st in leg at back of first sc on next Petal on **Fourth Posy**, ch 2, slip st in corresponding ch-5 sp on **First Posy** (first unworked ch-5 sp from sp joined to Second Posy), ch 2, slip st in leg at back of first sc on next Petal on **Fourth Posy**, ch 2, slip st in next ch-5 sp on **First Posy**, ch 2; working **below** first slip st on **Fourth Posy**, join with slip st to same leg as first slip st, finish off.

CENTER MOTIF

Rnd 1 (Right side): With Sport Weight Rose and smaller size hook, ch 2, 4 sc in second ch from hook; join with slip st to first sc.

Rnd 2 (Joining rnd): Ch 1, sc in same st, ch 1; with **right** side of joined Posies facing and working in sps at center, slip st in any sp; ★ † ch 1, sc in same st on **Center Motif**, ch 1, slip st in next sp on **Posies**, ch 1 †, sc in next sc on **Center Motif**, ch 1, slip st in next sp on **Posies**; repeat from ★ 2 times **more**, then repeat from † to † once; join with slip st to first sc on **Center Motif**, finish off.

BORDER

Rnd 1: With **right** side facing, larger size hook, and working in unworked ch-5 sps along outer edge of Posy Cluster, join Aran with slip st in marked ch-5 sp; ch 3 **(counts as first dc, now and throughout)**, (3 dc, tr) in same sp, ★ † ch 3, (tr, 4 dc) in next ch-5 sp, 4 dc in next ch-5 sp, dc decrease, 4 dc in same sp †, (4 dc, tr) in next ch-5 sp; repeat from ★ 2 times **more**, then repeat from † to † once; join with slip st to first dc: 76 sts and 4 ch-3 sps.

Rnd 2: Ch 3, dc in next dc and in each st around working (2 dc, ch 3, 2 dc) in each ch-3 sp; join with slip st to first dc: 92 dc and 4 ch-3 sps.

Rnd 3: Ch 1, sc in same st and in each dc around working 3 sc in each ch-3 sp; join with slip st to first sc, finish off: 104 sc.

ASSEMBLY
SQUARES

With Aran and working through inside loops only, whipstitch Squares together **(Fig. 21a, page 142)**, forming 6 strips of 6 Squares each, beginning in center sc of first corner 3-sc group and ending in center sc of next corner 3-sc group.

STRIPS

Note: For first Strip, work Edging and omit Trim; for remaining five Strips, work Edging and then add Trim across **one** long edge on each of these Strips.

EDGING

Rnd 1: With **right** side facing, larger size hook, and working in Back Loops Only **(Fig. 16, page 141)**, join Aran with sc in center sc of top right corner 3-sc group on one long edge **(see Joining With Sc, page 140)**; 2 sc in same st, † sc in next 25 sc, ★ sc in same st as joining on same Square and in same st as joining on next Square, sc in next 25 sc; repeat from ★ 4 times **more**, 3 sc in center sc of next corner 3-sc group, sc in next 25 sc †, 3 sc in center sc of next corner 3-sc group, repeat from † to † once; join with slip st to **both** loops of first sc, finish off: 382 sc.

TRIM

Row 1: With **right** side facing, larger size hook, and working in both loops of each sc across one long edge of Strip, join Aran with slip st in center sc of first corner 3-sc group; ch 3, dc in next sc and in each sc across working last dc in center sc of next corner 3-sc group; finish off: 164 dc.

Row 2: With **right** side facing and larger size hook, join Worsted Weight Rose with sc in first dc; sc decrease, sc in each dc across; finish off: 163 sc.

Row 3: With **right** side facing and larger size hook, join Aran with slip st in first sc and pull up a $1/2$" loop; work Puff St in same st, ★ ch 1, skip next sc, work Puff St in next sc; repeat from ★ across; finish off: 82 Puff Sts and 81 ch-1 sps.

Row 4: With **right** side facing and larger size hook, join Worsted Weight Rose with sc in first Puff St; sc in same st and in each ch-1 sp and each Puff St across; finish off: 164 sc.

Row 5: With **right** side facing and larger size hook, join Aran with slip st in first sc; ch 3, dc in next sc and in each sc across; finish off.

JOINING

Using photo as a guide for placement, arrange Strips to form Afghan with first Strip (without Trim) at **top** and remaining Strips **below** (with Trim at top of each Strip). With Aran, whipstitch Strips together, beginning and ending by matching center sc of corner 3-sc groups to dc at ends of Trim on adjacent Strips.

AFGHAN EDGING
FOUNDATION

Rnd 1: With **right** side facing, larger size hook, and working across one short edge, join Worsted Weight Rose with sc in center sc of first corner 3-sc group; 2 sc in same st, † sc decrease, sc in each sc across to center sc of next corner 3-sc group, 3 sc in center sc; working in sc on Squares and in end of rows on Trims, work 213 sc evenly spaced across to center sc of next corner 3-sc group †, 3 sc in center sc, repeat from † to † once; join with slip st to first sc, finish off: 760 sc.

Rnd 2: With **right** side facing and larger size hook, join Aran with sc in any sc; sc in each sc around working 3 sc in center sc of each corner 3-sc group; join with slip st to first sc, finish off: 217 sc on each long edge, 165 sc on each short edge, and 4 corner sc (768 sc total).

PANEL

Note: Work separate Panel on **each** side of Afghan. The center sc of each corner 3-sc group on Rnd 2 of Foundation will be left unworked.

Row 1: With **right** side facing and larger size hook, join Aran with sc in third sc of any corner 3-sc group; ★ ch 5, skip next 3 sc, sc in next sc; repeat from ★ across **one** side of Afghan working last sc in first sc of next corner 3-sc group.

Rows 2 and 3: Ch 5, turn; sc in first ch-5 sp, (ch 5, sc in next ch-5 sp) across.

Row 4: Ch 5, turn; sc in first ch-5 sp, (ch 5, sc in next ch-5 sp) across, place marker around last ch-5 made for st placement; finish off.

Repeat for remaining 3 sides.

CORNER POSY

Work same as First Posy of Posy Cluster, omitting marker: 8 ch-5 sps.

Rnd 5 (Joining rnd): With **right** side facing and larger size hook, join Aran with sc in any ch-5 sp; (ch 3, sc in next ch-5 sp) 3 times, ch 2; with **right** side of Afghan facing, sc in marked ch-5 sp on any Panel, remove marker, ch 2, † sc in next ch-5 sp on **Posy**, ch 2, sc in next sp on **Afghan**, ch 2 †, sc in next ch-5 sp on **Posy**, ch 2, sc in unworked center sc of corner 3-sc group on **Afghan**, ch 2, repeat from † to † twice; join with slip st to first sc, finish off. Repeat to add Corner Posy to each remaining corner on Afghan.

TRIM

Rnd 1: With **right** side facing, larger size hook, and working in sps on outer edges of Panels and Corner Posies, join Aran with sc in any sp; ch 5, slip st in third ch from hook, ch 2, ★ sc in next sp, ch 5, slip st in third ch from hook, ch 2; repeat from ★ around; join with slip st to first sc, finish off.

SUMMER

*Ahhh … the carefree days of summer — warm weather,
cool drinks, and plenty of time for fun and relaxation! We've
filled this section with a bounty of "sun-sational" seasonal afghans.
Many of them are worked either in squares or strips, so you can
take them along to crochet when you're out on the porch,
at the lake, at the ballpark, or even while on vacation.*

Sunrise

Brighten your morning with a blanket of sunshine. Each row is worked across the length of the afghan, and eyelet-forming star stitches give this heavenly wrap its radiant appeal.

Finished Size: 47^1/$_2$" x 63^1/$_2$"

MATERIALS
Worsted Weight Yarn:
- Yellow - 28 ounces, (800 grams, 1,635 yards)
- Lt Yellow - 14^1/$_4$ ounces, (410 grams, 830 yards)
- Blue - 9^1/$_4$ ounces, (270 grams, 540 yards)
- Crochet hook, size H (5.00 mm) **or** size needed for gauge

GAUGE: (Sc, ch 2) 3 times = 2^1/$_2$";
Rows 1-10 = 3^1/$_4$"

Gauge Swatch: 3^3/$_4$"w x 3^1/$_4$"h
Ch 13 **loosely**; finish off.
Work same as Afghan Rows 1-10.

STITCH GUIDE

BEGINNING STAR STITCH
(abbreviated Beginning Star St)
Pull up a loop in third ch from hook and in next ch, pull up a loop in first sc and in next 2 chs, YO and draw through all 6 loops on hook, ch 1 to close Beginning Star St and form eyelet.

STAR STITCH *(abbreviated Star St)*
Pull up a loop in top side loops and in bottom side loops of dc just made *(Fig. 1a)*, pull up a loop in same sc at base of dc and in next 2 chs, YO and draw through all 6 loops on hook *(Fig. 1b)*, ch 1 to close Star St and form eyelet *(Fig. 1c)*.

Fig. 1a

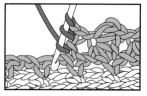

Fig. 1b

Fig. 1c

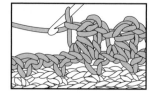

Note: Each row is worked across length of Afghan. When joining yarn and finishing off, leave an 8" end to be worked into fringe.

AFGHAN
With Blue, ch 229 **loosely**; finish off.

Row 1 (Right side): Working in back ridges of beginning ch *(Fig. 2b, page 137)*, join Lt Yellow with sc in first ch *(see Joining With Sc, page 140)*; ★ ch 2, skip next 2 chs, sc in next ch; repeat from ★ across; finish off: 77 sc and 76 ch-2 sps.

Note: Loop a short piece of yarn around any stitch to mark Row 1 as **right** side.

Row 2: With **wrong** side facing, join Yellow with sc in first sc; (ch 2, sc in next sc) across; do **not** finish off.

Row 3: Ch 4 **(counts as first dc plus ch 1)**, turn; work Beginning Star St, dc in next sc, ★ ch 1, work Star St, dc in next sc; repeat from ★ across; finish off.

Row 4: With **wrong** side facing, join Lt Yellow with sc in first dc; (ch 2, sc in next dc) across; finish off.

Row 5: With **right** side facing, join Blue with sc in first sc; (ch 2, sc in next sc) across; finish off.

Row 6: With **wrong** side facing, join Lt Yellow with sc in first sc; (ch 2, sc in next sc) across; finish off.

Rows 7-145: Repeat Rows 2-6, 27 times; then repeat Rows 2-5 once **more**.

Using photo as a guide for placement and holding a total of 8 strands of corresponding color yarn together, each 17" long, add fringe in end of rows across short edges of Afghan *(Figs. 22b & d, page 142)*.

American Spirit

*Express your proud American spirit by crocheting a rousing salute to
Old Glory! Squares of American flags create the patriotic wrap.*

Finished Size: 50" x 66"

MATERIALS
Worsted Weight Yarn:
   Red - 28$^1/_2$ ounces, (810 grams, 1,610 yards)
   White - 21 ounces, (600 grams, 1,190 yards)
   Blue - 11 ounces, (310 grams, 620 yards)
Crochet hook, size H (5.00 mm) **or** size needed for
   gauge
Yarn needle

GAUGE: Each Square = 8"

Gauge Swatch: 4"w x 2"h
Ch 15 **loosely**.
Row 1: Sc in second ch from hook and in each ch
across: 14 sc.
Rows 2-8: Ch 1, turn; sc in each sc across.
Finish off.

STITCH GUIDE

> **PUFF ST**
> ★ YO, insert hook in st indicated, YO and pull
> up a loop; repeat from ★ once **more**, YO and
> draw through all 5 loops on hook *(Fig. 13,
> page 139)*.

To work **color change**, work the last st to within one
step of completion, drop yarn, hook new yarn and
draw through all loops on hook *(Fig. 19, page 141)*.
Do **not** cut yarn unless otherwise instructed.

SQUARE (Make 48)
CENTER
With Blue, ch 6 **loosely**, drop Blue, with Red, YO
and draw through loop on hook, ch 13 **loosely**:
20 chs.
Row 1: Sc in second ch from hook and in next 11 chs
changing to Blue in last sc, sc in last 7 chs: 19 sc.
Note: Continue to change colors in same manner.
Row 2 (Right side): Ch 1, turn; sc in first 7 sc, with
Red sc in last 12 sc changing to White in last sc.
Note: Loop a short piece of yarn around any stitch
to mark Row 2 as **right** side and top edge.
Row 3: Ch 1, turn; sc in first 12 sc, with Blue sc in
last 7 sc.

Row 4: Ch 1, turn; sc in first 7 sc, with White sc in
last 12 sc changing to Red in last sc.
Row 5: Ch 1, turn; sc in first 12 sc, with Blue sc in
last 7 sc.
Row 6: Ch 1, turn; sc in first 7 sc, with Red sc in last
12 sc changing to White in last sc.
Rows 7-10: Repeat Rows 3-6.
Cut Blue.
Row 11: Ch 1, turn; sc in each sc across.
Row 12: Ch 1, turn; sc in each sc across changing to
Red in last sc.
Row 13: Ch 1, turn; sc in each sc across.
Row 14: Ch 1, turn; sc in each sc across changing to
White in last sc.
Rows 15-21: Repeat Rows 11-14 once, then repeat
Rows 11-13 once **more**.
Cut White.
Row 22: Ch 1, turn; sc in each sc across; finish off.

BORDER
Rnd 1: With **right** side facing, join Blue with sc in last
sc on Row 22 *(see Joining With Sc, page 140)*; 2 sc in
same st, work 17 sc evenly spaced across end of rows;
working in free loops of beginning ch *(Fig. 17b,
page 141)*, 3 sc in ch at base of first sc, sc in each ch
across to last ch, 3 sc in last ch; work 17 sc evenly
spaced across end of rows; working in sts across
Row 22, 3 sc in first sc, sc in next sc and in each sc
across; join with slip st to first sc, finish off: 80 sc.
Rnd 2: With **right** side facing, join White with slip st
in center sc of any corner 3-sc group; ch 1, work
(Puff St, ch 2, Puff St) in same st, ch 1, skip next sc,
(work Puff St in next sc, ch 1, skip next sc) across to
center sc of next corner 3-sc group, ★ work (Puff St,
ch 2, Puff St) in center sc, ch 1, skip next sc, (work
Puff St in next sc, ch 1, skip next sc) across to center
sc of next corner 3-sc group; repeat from ★ 2 times
more; join with slip st to top of first Puff St,
finish off: 44 sps.
Rnd 3: With **right** side facing, join Red with slip st in
any corner ch-2 sp; ch 2 **(counts as first hdc, now
and throughout)**, 4 hdc in same sp, ★ 2 hdc in each
ch-1 sp across to next corner ch-2 sp, 5 hdc in corner
ch-2 sp; repeat from ★ 2 times **more**, 2 hdc in each
ch-1 sp across; join with slip st to first hdc, finish off:
100 hdc.

Continued on page 44.

ASSEMBLY

With Red, keeping top edges toward same end, and working through both loops, whipstitch Squares together (*Fig. 21b, page 142*), forming 6 vertical strips of 8 Squares each, beginning in center hdc of first corner 5-hdc group and ending in center hdc of next corner 5-hdc group; whipstitch strips together in same manner.

EDGING

Rnd 1: With **right** side facing, join Red with sc in center hdc of any corner 5-hdc group; sc in same st and in each hdc and each joining across to center hdc of next corner 5-hdc group, ★ 3 sc in center hdc, sc in each hdc and in each joining across to center hdc of next corner 5-hdc group; repeat from ★ 2 times **more**, sc in same st as first sc; join with slip st to first sc: 708 sc.
Rnd 2: Ch 1, work (Puff St, ch 2, Puff St) in same st, ch 1, skip next sc, (work Puff St in next sc, ch 1, skip next sc) across to center sc of next corner 3-sc group, ★ work (Puff St, ch 2, Puff St) in center sc, ch 1, skip next sc, (work Puff St in next sc, ch 1, skip next sc) across to center sc of next corner 3-sc group; repeat from ★ 2 times **more**; join with slip st to first Puff St.
Rnd 3: Slip st in first ch-2 sp, ch 2, 4 hdc in same sp, ★ 2 hdc in each ch-1 sp across to next corner ch-2 sp, 5 hdc in corner ch-2 sp; repeat from ★ 2 times **more**, 2 hdc in each ch-1 sp across; join with slip st to first hdc, finish off.

Bride's Dream

Honor that special bride on her wedding day with a handmade gift of love. As light as a dream, the fringed afghan will be cherished from this day forward.

Finished Size: 48" x 65$\frac{1}{2}$"

MATERIALS
Worsted Weight Yarn:
45 ounces, (1,280 grams, 2,545 yards)
Crochet hook, size H (5.00 mm) **or** size needed for gauge

GAUGE: In pattern, 14 sc = 4"; 6 rows = 2$\frac{3}{4}$"

Gauge Swatch: 5"w x 3$\frac{1}{2}$"h
Ch 18 **loosely.**
Work same as Afghan for 9 rows.
Finish off.

STITCH GUIDE

> **PUFF ST**
> ★ YO, insert hook from **front** to **back** around post of last dc made (*Fig. 10, page 139*), YO and pull up a loop even with last dc made; repeat from ★ 3 times **more**, YO and draw through all 9 loops on hook (*Fig. 13, page 139*).

Note: Each row is worked across length of Afghan.

AFGHAN
Ch 230 **loosely.**
Row 1 (Right side): Sc in back ridge of second ch from hook (*Fig. 2b, page 137*) and each ch across: 229 sc.

Note: Loop a short piece of yarn around any stitch to mark Row 1 as **right** side.
Rows 2 and 3: Ch 1, turn; sc in each sc across.
Row 4: Ch 4 **(counts as first dc plus ch 1, now and throughout)**, turn; skip next sc, dc in next sc, ★ ch 1, skip next sc, dc in next sc; repeat from ★ across: 115 dc and 114 ch-1 sps.
Row 5: Ch 4, turn; dc in next dc, ch 1, work Puff St, ★ (dc in next dc, ch 1) twice, work Puff St; repeat from ★ across to last dc, dc in last dc: 57 Puff Sts and 114 ch-1 sps.
Row 6: Ch 4, turn; dc in ch-1 sp **above** next Puff St, ch 1, ★ dc in next ch-1, ch 1, dc in ch-1 sp **above** next Puff St, ch 1; repeat from ★ across to last ch-1 sp, skip last ch-1 sp, dc in last dc: 115 dc and 114 ch-1 sps.
Row 7: Ch 1, turn; sc in each dc and in each ch-1 sp across: 229 sc.
Rows 8 and 9: Ch 1, turn; sc in each sc across.
Row 10: Ch 4, turn; skip next sc, dc in next sc, ★ ch 1, skip next sc, dc in next sc; repeat from ★ across: 115 dc and 114 ch-1 sps.
Repeat Rows 5-10 until Afghan measures approximately 48" from beginning ch, ending by working Row 9.
Finish off.

Using photo as a guide and holding 8 strands of yarn together, each 16" long, add fringe across short edges of Afghan (*Figs. 22b & d, page 142*).

Lavender & Lace

Crocheted in the soothing shade of lavender, this lacy afghan offers a genteel touch.
The lightweight throw is ideal for quiet summer afternoons of daydreaming.

Finished Size: 47" x 64"

MATERIALS
Worsted Weight Yarn:
   33 ounces, (940 grams, 2,260 yards)
Crochet hook, size J (6.00 mm) **or** size needed for
gauge

GAUGE: In pattern, 2 repeats and 8 rows = 5"

Gauge Swatch: 6"w x 5"h
Ch 22.
Work same as Afghan Body for 8 rows.
Finish off.

STITCH GUIDE

> **DECREASE** (uses next 5 sts)
> Pull up a loop in next dc, skip next 3 sts, pull up
> a loop in next dc, YO and draw through all
> 3 loops on hook.

AFGHAN BODY
Ch 102.
Row 1 (Right side): Dc in sixth ch from hook
(5 skipped chs count as first dc plus ch 2), ★ skip
next 3 chs, 5 dc in next ch, skip next 3 chs, (dc, ch 2,
dc) in next ch; repeat from ★ across: 86 dc and
13 ch-2 sps.
Row 2: Ch 3 **(counts as first dc, now and
throughout),** turn; 2 dc in first ch-2 sp, (dc, ch 2, dc)
in center dc of next 5-dc group, ★ 5 dc in next
ch-2 sp, (dc, ch 2, dc) in center dc of next 5-dc group;
repeat from ★ across to last ch-2 sp, 2 dc in last
ch-2 sp, dc in last dc: 85 dc and 12 ch-2 sps.
Row 3: Ch 5 **(counts as first dc plus ch 2, now and
throughout),** turn; dc in same st, 5 dc in next
ch-2 sp, ★ (dc, ch 2, dc) in center dc of next
5-dc group, 5 dc in next ch-2 sp; repeat from ★
across to last 4 dc, skip next 3 dc, (dc, ch 2, dc) in
last dc: 86 dc and 13 ch-2 sps.
Repeat Rows 2 and 3 until Afghan Body measures
approximately 48" from beginning ch, ending by
working Row 2; do **not** finish off.

EDGING
Rnd 1: Ch 1, turn; sc in first 4 dc, 2 sc in next
ch-2 sp, (sc in next 7 dc and in next ch-2 sp) 5 times,
sc in next 3 dc, 2 sc in next dc, sc in next 3 dc, (sc in
next ch-2 sp and in next 7 dc) across to last ch-2 sp,
2 sc in last ch-2 sp, sc in last 4 dc, place marker
around last sc made for st placement; work 152 sc
evenly spaced across end of rows; working in free
loops *(Fig. 17b, page 141)* and in sps across
beginning ch, sc in first ch, place marker around sc
just made for st placement, 4 sc in next sp, (sc in
next ch, 3 sc in next sp) 11 times, 2 sc in next ch, (3 sc
in next sp, sc in next ch) across to last sp, 4 sc in last
sp, sc in next ch, place marker around sc just made
for st placement; work 152 sc evenly spaced across
end of rows; join with slip st to first sc: 504 sc.
Rnd 2: Ch 5, do **not** turn; skip next 2 sc, ★ (dc in
next sc, ch 2, skip next 2 sc) across to next marked
sc, (dc, ch 3, dc) in marked sc, ch 2, skip next 2 sc;
repeat from ★ 2 times **more,** (dc in next sc, ch 2, skip
next 2 sc) across, dc in same st as first dc, ch 1, hdc
in first dc to form last ch-3 sp: 172 dc and 172 sps.
Rnd 3: Ch 5, ★ (dc in next dc, ch 2) across to next
corner ch-3 sp, (dc, ch 3, dc) in corner ch-3 sp, ch 2;
repeat from ★ 2 times **more,** (dc in next dc, ch 2)
across, dc in same sp as first dc, ch 1, hdc in first dc
to form last ch-3 sp: 180 dc and 180 sps.
Rnd 4: Ch 1, 2 sc in last ch-3 sp made, (sc in next dc,
2 sc in next ch-2 sp) across to within one dc of next
corner ch-3 sp, 2 sc in next dc, ★ 3 sc in corner
ch-3 sp, (sc in next dc, 2 sc in next ch-2 sp) across to
within one dc of next corner ch-3 sp, 2 sc in next dc;
repeat from ★ 2 times **more,** sc in same sp as first sc;
join with slip st to first sc: 548 sc.
Rnd 5: Ch 1, sc in same st and in next 2 sc, ch 5,
(skip next 3 sc, sc in next 3 sc, ch 5) across to within
4 sc of next corner 3-sc group, skip next 3 sc, sc in
next 2 sc, ★ (sc, ch 5, sc) in next sc, sc in next 2 sc,
ch 5, (skip next 3 sc, sc in next 3 sc, ch 5) across to
within 4 sc of next corner 3-sc group, skip next 3 sc,
sc in next 2 sc; repeat from ★ 2 times **more,** sc in
same st as first sc, ch 2, dc in first sc to form last
ch-5 sp: 94 ch-5 sps.

Continued on page 48.

Rnd 6: Ch 3, 4 dc in last ch-5 sp made, sc in center sc of next 3-sc group, (7 dc in next ch-5 sp, sc in center sc of next 3-sc group) across to next corner ch-5 sp, ★ 9 dc in corner ch-5 sp, sc in center sc of next 3-sc group, (7 dc in next ch-5 sp, sc in center sc of next 3-sc group) across to next corner ch-5 sp; repeat from ★ 2 times **more**, 4 dc in same sp as first dc; join with slip st to first dc: 94 dc groups and 94 sc.

Rnd 7: Ch 5, skip next dc, dc in next dc, ch 2, ★ † decrease, ch 2, [skip next dc, (dc, ch 2) twice in next dc, skip next dc, decrease, ch 2] across to third dc of next corner 9-dc group, dc in next dc, ch 2, skip next dc †, (dc, ch 2) twice in next dc, skip next dc, dc in next dc, ch 2; repeat from ★ 2 times **more**, then repeat from † to † once, dc in same st as first dc, ch 1, sc in first dc to form last ch-2 sp: 290 ch-2 sps.

Rnd 8: Ch 1, sc in last ch-2 sp made, ★ † 2 sc in next ch-2 sp, ch 5, (skip next 2 ch-2 sps, 3 sc in next ch-2 sp, ch 5) across to within 3 ch-2 sps of next corner ch-2 sp, skip next 2 ch-2 sps, 2 sc in next ch-2 sp †, (sc, ch 5, sc) in corner ch-2 sp; repeat from ★ 2 times **more**, then repeat from † to † once, sc in same sp as first sc, ch 2, dc in first sc to form last ch-5 sp: 98 ch-5 sps.

Rnds 9-15: Repeat Rnds 6-8 twice, then repeat Rnd 6 once **more**: 106 dc groups and 106 sc.

Rnd 16: Ch 1, (sc, ch 5, sc) in same st, ★ † ch 3, sc in next dc, ch 3, skip next dc, decrease, ch 3, [skip next dc, (sc, ch 5, sc) in next dc, ch 3, skip next dc, decrease, ch 3] across to third dc of next corner 9-dc group, skip next dc, sc in next dc, ch 3 †, (sc, ch 5, sc) in next dc; repeat from ★ 2 times **more**, then repeat from † to † once; join with slip st to first sc, finish off.

Star-Spangled Banner

"Oh, say, does that Star-Spangled Banner yet wave o'er the land of the free and the home of the brave?" Yes! Commemorate America's unwavering courage with this Stars & Stripes throw.

Finished Size: 52^1/$_2$" x 70"

MATERIALS

Worsted Weight Yarn:
   Red - 30 ounces, (850 grams, 1,695 yards)
   White - 26 ounces, (740 grams, 1,470 yards)
   Blue - 11^1/$_2$ ounces, (330 grams, 650 yards)
   Gold - 3 ounces, (90 grams, 170 yards)
Crochet hooks, sizes F (3.75 mm) **and** H (5.00 mm)
   or sizes needed for gauge
Yarn needle

GAUGE: With larger size hook, 14 dc and
            7 rows = 4"

Gauge Swatch: 4" square
With larger size hook and Red, ch 16 **loosely**.
Row 1: Dc in fourth ch from hook **(3 skipped chs count as first dc)** and in each ch across: 14 dc.
Rows 2-7: Ch 3 **(counts as first dc)**, turn; dc in next dc and in each dc across.
Finish off.

STITCH GUIDE

FRONT POST DOUBLE CROCHET
   (abbreviated FPdc)
YO, insert hook from **front** to **back** around post of st indicated *(Fig. 10, page 139)*, YO and pull up a loop even with loop on hook (3 loops on hook), (YO and draw through 2 loops on hook) twice.

BACK POST DOUBLE CROCHET
   (abbreviated BPdc)
YO, insert hook from **back** to **front** around post of st indicated *(Fig. 10, page 139)*, YO and pull up a loop even with loop on hook (3 loops on hook), (YO and draw through 2 loops on hook) twice.

Continued on page 50.

To work **color change**, work the last st to within one step of completion, drop yarn, hook new yarn and draw through all loops on hook *(Fig. 19, page 141)*. Do **not** cut yarn unless otherwise instructed.

Note: Each row is worked across length of Afghan.

AFGHAN BODY

With larger size hook and Red, ch 245 **loosely**.

Row 1 (Right side): Dc in fourth ch from hook **(3 skipped chs count as first dc)** and in each ch across: 243 dc.

Note: Loop a short piece of yarn around any stitch to mark Row 1 as **right** side.

Row 2: Ch 3 **(counts as first dc, now and throughout)**, turn; ★ work BPdc around next dc, skip dc behind BPdc, dc in next dc; repeat from ★ across.

Row 3: Ch 3, turn; (work FPdc around next BPdc, dc in next dc) across.

Row 4: Ch 3, turn; (work BPdc around next FPdc, dc in next dc) across.

Rows 5-7: Repeat Rows 3 and 4 once, then repeat Row 3 once **more**; at end of Row 7, finish off.

Row 8: With **wrong** side facing and using larger size hook, join White with dc in first dc *(see Joining With Dc, page 140)*; (work BPdc around next FPdc, dc in next dc) across.

Row 9: Ch 3, turn; (work FPdc around next BPdc, dc in next dc) across.

Row 10: Ch 3, turn; (work BPdc around next FPdc, dc in next dc) across.

Rows 11-14: Repeat Rows 9 and 10 twice; at end of last row, finish off.

Row 15: With **right** side facing and using larger size hook, join Red with dc in first dc; (work FPdc around next BPdc, dc in next dc) across.

Row 16: Ch 3, turn; (work BPdc around next FPdc, dc in next dc) across.

Row 17: Ch 3, turn; (work FPdc around next BPdc, dc in next dc) across.

Rows 18-21: Repeat Rows 16 and 17 twice; at end of last row, finish off.

Rows 22-49: Repeat Rows 8-21 twice.

Row 50: With **wrong** side facing and using larger size hook, join Blue with dc in first dc; dc in next 107 sts changing to White in last dc made, do **not** cut Blue; dc in next dc, (work BPdc around next FPdc, dc in next dc) across.

Row 51: Ch 3, turn; (work FPdc around next BPdc, dc in next dc) 67 times changing to Blue in last dc made; dc in each dc across.

Row 52: Ch 3, turn; dc in next 107 dc changing to White in last dc made; dc in next dc, (work BPdc around next FPdc, dc in next dc) across.

Rows 53-56: Repeat Rows 51 and 52 twice; at end of last row, finish off White.

Row 57: With **right** side facing and using larger size hook, join Red with dc in first dc; (work FPdc around next BPdc, dc in next dc) 67 times changing to Blue in last dc made; dc in each dc across.

Row 58: Ch 3, turn; dc in next 107 dc changing to Red in last dc made; dc in next dc, (work BPdc around next FPdc, dc in next dc) across.

Row 59: Ch 3, turn; (work FPdc around next BPdc, dc in next dc) 67 times changing to Blue in last dc made; dc in each dc across.

Rows 60-63: Repeat Rows 58 and 59 twice; at end of last row, cut Red.

Row 64: Ch 3, turn; dc in next 107 dc changing to White in last dc made; dc in next dc, (work BPdc around next FPdc, dc in next dc) across.

Rows 65-91: Repeat Rows 51-64 once, then repeat Rows 51-63 once **more**.

Finish off.

EDGING

Rnd 1: With **right** side facing and using larger size hook, join Gold with sc in any corner *(see Joining With Sc, page 140)*; sc evenly around working 3 sc in each corner; join with slip st to first sc.

Rnd 2: Ch 1, do **not** turn; sc in each sc around working 3 sc in center sc of each corner 3-sc group; join with slip st to first sc, finish off.

STARS (Make 50)

With smaller size hook and White, ch 6; join with slip st to form a ring.

Rnd 1: (Hdc, dc, tr, ch 5, slip st) 5 times in ring; finish off.

Using photo as a guide for placement, sew Stars to **right** side of Blue field.

Tropical Delight

Bursting with color, this afghan is a tropical delight! Drape it over a sofa or chair, then sit back and imagine yourself on a quiet, secluded island.

Finished Size: 45¹/₂" x 60³/₄"

MATERIALS
Worsted Weight Yarn:
    Variegated - 20 ounces, (570 grams, 1,210 yards)
    Lavender - 11¹/₂ ounces, (330 grams, 650 yards)
    Lt Mint - 11¹/₂ ounces, (330 grams, 650 yards)
    Lilac - 5¹/₂ ounces, (160 grams, 310 yards)
    Lt Teal - 5¹/₂ ounces, (160 grams, 310 yards)
Crochet hook, size I (5.50 mm) **or** size needed for gauge
Yarn needle

GAUGE: Center = 3¹/₄"w x 3¹/₂"h
            Each Motif = 6¹/₂"w x 6³/₄"h

STITCH GUIDE

> **CLUSTER** (uses one sc)
> ★ YO, insert hook in sc indicated, YO and pull up a loop, YO and draw through 2 loops on hook; repeat from ★ 2 times **more**, YO and draw through all 4 loops on hook (*Figs. 11a & b, page 139*).

MOTIF A (Make 32)
CENTER
With Variegated, ch 12 **loosely**.
Row 1 (Right side): Sc in second ch from hook and in each ch across: 11 sc.
Note: Loop a short piece of yarn around any stitch on Row 1 to mark **right** side and bottom edge.
Row 2: Ch 1, turn; sc in first sc, (work Cluster in next sc, sc in next sc) across: 6 sc and 5 Clusters.
Row 3: Ch 1, turn; sc in each st across: 11 sc.
Row 4: Ch 1, turn; sc in first sc, work Cluster in next sc, sc in next sc, (tr in next sc, sc in next sc) 3 times, work Cluster in next sc, sc in last sc: 6 sc, 3 tr, and 2 Clusters.
Row 5: Ch 1, turn; sc in each st across: 11 sc.
Rows 6-9: Repeat Rows 4 and 5 twice.
Row 10: Ch 1, turn; sc in first sc, (work Cluster in next sc, sc in next sc) across: 6 sc and 5 Clusters.
Row 11: Ch 1, turn; sc in each st across; finish off: 11 sc.

BORDER
Rnd 1: With **right** side facing, join Lavender with sc in first sc (*see Joining With Sc, page 140*); 2 sc in same st, sc in next 9 sc, 3 sc in last sc; work 10 sc evenly spaced across end of rows; working in free loops of beginning ch (*Fig. 17b, page 141*), 3 sc in first ch, sc next 9 chs, 3 sc in next ch; work 10 sc evenly spaced across end of rows; join with slip st to first sc: 50 sc.
Rnd 2: Ch 1, turn; sc in same st, ★ sc in each sc across to center sc of next corner 3-sc group, (sc, ch 2, sc) in center sc; repeat from ★ around; join with slip st to first sc, finish off: 54 sc and 4 ch-2 sps.
Rnd 3: With **right** side facing, join Lt Mint with sc in any corner ch-2 sp; ch 2, sc in same sp, ★ sc in each sc across to next corner ch-2 sp, (sc, ch 2, sc) in corner ch-2 sp; repeat from ★ 2 times **more**, sc in each sc across; join with slip st to first sc: 62 sc and 4 ch-2 sps.
Rnd 4: Ch 1, turn; sc in same st, ★ sc in each sc across to next corner ch-2 sp, (sc, ch 2, sc) in corner ch-2 sp; repeat from ★ around; join with slip st to first sc, finish off: 70 sc and 4 ch-2 sps.
Rnd 5: With **right** side facing, join Lavender with sc in any corner ch-2 sp; ch 2, sc in same sp, ★ sc in each sc across to next corner ch-2 sp, (sc, ch 2, sc) in corner ch-2 sp; repeat from ★ 2 times **more**, sc in each sc across; join with slip st to first sc: 78 sc and 4 ch-2 sps.
Rnd 6: Ch 1, turn; sc in same st, ★ sc in each sc across to next corner ch-2 sp, (sc, ch 2, sc) in corner ch-2 sp; repeat from ★ around; join with slip st to first sc, finish off: 86 sc and 4 ch-2 sps.
Rnd 7: With **right** side facing, join Variegated with sc in any corner ch-2 sp; 2 sc in same sp, ★ sc in each sc across to next corner ch-2 sp, 3 sc in corner ch-2 sp; repeat from ★ 2 times **more**, sc in each sc across; join with slip st to first sc, finish off: 98 sc.

Continued on page 52.

MOTIF B (Make 31)

CENTER

Work same as Motif A.

BORDER

Rnd 1: With **right** side facing, join Lilac with sc in first sc; 2 sc in same st, sc in next 9 sc, 3 sc in last sc; work 10 sc evenly spaced across end of rows; working in free loops of beginning ch, 3 sc in first ch, sc next 9 chs, 3 sc in next ch; work 10 sc evenly spaced across end of rows; join with slip st to first sc: 50 sc.

Rnd 2: Ch 1, turn; sc in same st, ★ sc in each sc across to center sc of next corner 3-sc group, (sc, ch 2, sc) in center sc; repeat from ★ around; join with slip st to first sc, finish off: 54 sc and 4 ch-2 sps.

Rnd 3: With **right** side facing, join Lt Teal with sc in any corner ch-2 sp; ch 2, sc in same sp, ★ sc in each sc across to next corner ch-2 sp, (sc, ch 2, sc) in corner ch-2 sp; repeat from ★ 2 times **more**, sc in each sc across; join with slip st to first sc: 62 sc and 4 ch-2 sps.

Rnd 4: Ch 1, turn; sc in same st, ★ sc in each sc across to next corner ch-2 sp, (sc, ch 2, sc) in corner ch-2 sp; repeat from ★ around; join with slip st to first sc, finish off: 70 sc and 4 ch-2 sps.

Rnd 5: With **right** side facing, join Lilac with sc in any ch-2 sp; ch 2, sc in same sp, ★ sc in each sc across to next corner ch-2 sp, (sc, ch 2, sc) in corner ch-2 sp; repeat from ★ 2 times **more**, sc in each sc across; join with slip st to first sc: 78 sc and 4 ch-2 sps.

Rnd 6: Ch 1, turn; sc in same st, ★ sc in each sc across to next corner ch-2 sp, (sc, ch 2, sc) in corner ch-2 sp; repeat from ★ around; join with slip st to first sc, finish off: 86 sc and 4 ch-2 sps.

Rnd 7: With **right** side facing, join Variegated with sc in any corner ch-2 sp; 2 sc in same sp, ★ sc in each sc across to next corner ch-2 sp, 3 sc in corner ch-2 sp; repeat from ★ 2 times **more**, sc in each sc across; join with slip st to first sc, finish off: 98 sc.

FINISHING

ASSEMBLY

With Variegated and using Placement Diagram as a guide, whipstitch Motifs together as instructed, forming 7 vertical strips of 9 Motifs each, beginning in center sc of first corner 3-sc group and ending in center sc of next corner 3-sc group; whipstitch strips together in same manner.

WHIPSTITCH

Place two Motifs with **wrong** sides facing, bottom edges at same end, and matching stitches. Beginning in first corner sc, sew through **both** Motifs to secure beginning of seam, leaving an ample yarn end to weave in later, ★ insert needle from **right** to **left** in horizontal bar of next sc on both pieces and pull yarn through (*Figs. 1a & b*); repeat from ★ across to next corner sc.

Fig. 1a

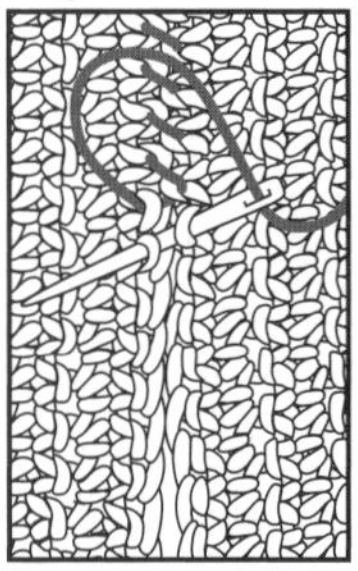

(wrong side)

Fig. 1b

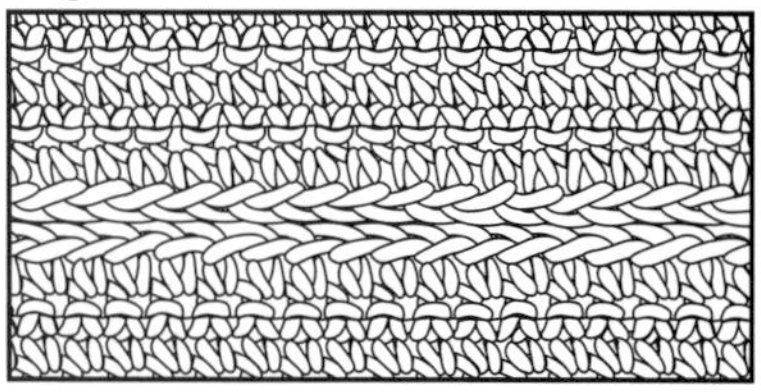

(right side)

PLACEMENT DIAGRAM

A	B	A	B	A	B	A
B	A	B	A	B	A	B
A	B	A	B	A	B	A
B	A	B	A	B	A	B
A	B	A	B	A	B	A
B	A	B	A	B	A	B
A	B	A	B	A	B	A
B	A	B	A	B	A	B
A	B	A	B	A	B	A

Elegant Ivy

Like endless garden paths lined with ivy, the strips in this elegant afghan are defined by their classic borders. The soft throw will make a nice accent for the patio or a garden room.

Finished Size: 55" x 71"

MATERIALS
  Worsted Weight Yarn:
    Green - 36 ounces, (1,020 grams, 2,365 yards)
    Dk Green - 19 ounces, (540 grams, 1,250 yards)
  Crochet hook, size H (5.00 mm) **or** size needed for gauge
  Yarn needle

GAUGE: Each Strip = 5" wide

Gauge Swatch: $2^1/4$"w x $3^3/4$"h
Work same as Center through Row 5.
Finish off.

STRIP (Make 11)
CENTER
With Green, ch 11 **loosely**.
Row 1 (Right side): Dc in fourth ch from hook **(3 skipped chs count as first dc)**, skip next 2 chs, (3 dc, ch 1, 3 dc) in next ch, skip next 2 chs, dc in next ch, ch 2, slip st in last ch: 9 dc and one ch-2 sp.
Note: Loop a short piece of yarn around any stitch to mark Row 1 as **right** side and bottom edge.
Row 2: Ch 3 **(counts as first dc, now and throughout)**, do **not** turn; working in free loops of beginning ch **(Fig. 17b, page 141)**, dc in next ch, skip next 2 chs, (3 dc, ch 1, 3 dc) in next ch, skip next 2 chs, dc in next 2 chs: 10 dc and one ch-1 sp.
Rows 3-102: Ch 3, **turn**; dc in next dc, skip next 3 dc, (3 dc, ch 1, 3 dc) in next ch-1 sp, skip next 3 dc, dc in last 2 dc.
Finish off.

BORDER
Rnd 1: With **right** side facing and working in end of rows, join Dk Green with sc in ch-2 sp on Row 1 **(see Joining With Sc, page 140)**; ch 3, (sc in next row, ch 3) across; working across Row 102, skip first 2 dc, (sc in sp **before** next dc, ch 3, skip next 2 dc) 4 times **(Fig. 20, page 141)**; working in end of rows, sc in first row, ch 3, (sc in next row, ch 3) across; working across Row 1, skip first 2 dc, sc in sp **before** next dc, (ch 3, skip next 2 dc, sc in sp **before** next dc) 3 times, ch 1, skip last dc, hdc in first sc to form last ch-3 sp: 212 ch-3 sps.

Rnd 2: Ch 1, sc in last ch-3 sp made, ch 3, (sc in next ch-3 sp, ch 3) around; join with slip st to first sc, finish off.
Rnd 3: With **right** side facing, join Green with slip st in first ch-3 sp; ch 3, dc in same sp, ch 1, (2 dc in next ch-3 sp, ch 1) 101 times, † 3 dc in next ch-3 sp, ch 1, (4 dc in next ch-3 sp, ch 1) twice, 3 dc in next ch-3 sp, ch 1 †, (2 dc in next ch-3 sp, ch 1) 102 times, repeat from † to † once; join with slip st to first dc, finish off: 436 dc and 212 ch-1 sps.
Rnd 4: With **right** side facing, join Dk Green with sc in same st as joining; sc in Back Loop Only of next dc **(Fig. 16, page 141)**, working in **front** of next ch-1 **(Fig. 18, page 141)**, tr in **both** loops of sc one rnd **below** ch-1, place marker around tr just made for joining placement, † (sc in Back Loop Only of next 2 dc, working in **front** of next ch-1, tr in **both** loops of sc one rnd **below** ch-1) 100 times, place marker around last tr made for joining placement, sc in Back Loop Only of next 2 dc, working in **front** of next ch-1, tr in **both** loops of sc one rnd **below** ch-1, sc in Back Loop Only of next 3 dc, working in **front** of next ch-1, tr in **both** loops of sc one rnd **below** ch-1, (sc in Back Loop Only of next 4 dc, working in **front** of next ch-1, tr in **both** loops of sc one rnd **below** ch-1) twice, sc in Back Loop Only of next 3 dc, working in **front** of next ch-1, tr in **both** loops of sc one rnd **below** ch-1 †, sc in Back Loop Only of next 2 dc, working in **front** of next ch-1, tr in **both** loops of sc one rnd **below** ch-1, place marker around tr just made for joining placement, repeat from † to † once; join with slip st to **both** loops of first sc, finish off.

ASSEMBLY
With Dk Green and working through inside loops only, whipstitch Strips together **(Fig. 21a, page 142)**, beginning in first marked tr and ending in next marked tr.

Idyllic Day

Simplistic in nature, this pleasing wrap is ideal for picnics in the park. Cluster stitches produce the comforting texture while picots form a complementary edging.

Finished Size: 50" x 67"

MATERIALS
Worsted Weight Yarn:
    64 ounces, (1,820 grams, 3,735 yards)
Crochet hook, size G (4.00 mm) **or** size needed for gauge

GAUGE: In pattern, 2 repeats and 10 rows = 4"

Gauge Swatch: $4^1/_4$"w x 4"h
Ch 18 **loosely**.
Work same as Afghan Body for 10 rows.
Finish off.

STITCH GUIDE

CLUSTER (uses one st or sp)
★ YO, insert hook in st or sp indicated, YO and pull up a loop, YO and draw through 2 loops on hook; repeat from ★ 3 times **more**, YO and draw through all 5 loops on hook (*Figs. 11a & b, page 139*).
PICOT
Ch 3, slip st in top of sc just made (*Fig. 1*).

Fig. 1

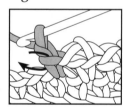

AFGHAN BODY
Ch 194 **loosely**.
Row 1: Sc in second ch from hook, ch 4, skip next 3 chs, work Cluster in next ch, ch 5, ★ skip next 3 chs, (sc, ch 1, sc) in next ch, ch 4, skip next 3 chs, work Cluster in next ch, ch 5; repeat from ★ across to last 4 chs, skip next 3 chs, sc in last ch: 24 Clusters and 71 sps.
Row 2 (Right side): Ch 3 **(counts as first dc)**, turn; 2 dc in same st, ch 2, sc in next Cluster, ch 2, ★ 6 dc in next ch-1 sp, ch 2, sc in next Cluster, ch 2; repeat from ★ across to last sc, 3 dc in last sc: 144 dc and 48 ch-2 sps.

Row 3: Ch 7 **(counts as first dc plus ch 4, now and throughout)**, turn; skip next 2 dc, (sc, ch 1, sc) in next sc, ch 4, ★ skip next 3 dc, work Cluster in sp **before** next dc (*Fig. 20, page 141*), ch 5, (sc, ch 1, sc) in next sc, ch 4; repeat from ★ across to last 3 dc, skip next 2 dc, dc in last dc: 23 Clusters and 72 sps.
Row 4: Ch 1, turn; sc in first dc, ch 2, 6 dc in next ch-1 sp, ch 2, ★ sc in next Cluster, ch 2, 6 dc in next ch-1 sp, ch 2; repeat from ★ across to last dc, sc in last dc: 144 dc and 48 ch-2 sps.
Row 5: Ch 1, turn; sc in first sc, ch 4, skip next 3 dc, work Cluster in sp **before** next dc, ch 5, ★ (sc, ch 1, sc) in next sc, ch 4, skip next 3 dc, work Cluster in sp **before** next dc, ch 5; repeat from ★ across to last sc, sc in last sc: 24 Clusters and 71 sps.
Rows 6-161: Repeat Rows 2-5, 39 times.
Row 162: Ch 7, turn; sc in next Cluster, ch 3, ★ sc in next ch-1 sp, ch 3, sc in next Cluster, ch 3; repeat from ★ across to last sc, dc in last sc; do **not** finish off: 49 sts and 48 sps.

EDGING
Rnd 1: Ch 1, do **not** turn; 2 sc in last dc on Row 162; work 259 sc evenly spaced across end of rows; working in sps and in free loops across beginning ch (*Fig. 17b, page 141*), 3 sc in ch at base of first sc and in next sp, (sc in next ch, 3 sc in next sp) across to last ch, 3 sc in last ch; work 259 sc evenly spaced across end of rows; working in sts and in sps on Row 162, 3 sc in first dc and in next sp, (sc in next sc, 3 sc in next sp) across, sc in same st as first sc; join with slip st to first sc: 912 sc.
Rnd 2: Ch 1, sc in same st, ch 3, ★ skip next sc, (sc in next sc, ch 3, skip next sc) across to center sc of next corner 3-sc group, (sc, ch 3) twice in center sc; repeat from ★ 2 times **more**, skip next sc, (sc in next sc, ch 3, skip next sc) across, sc in same st as first sc, ch 1, hdc in first sc to form last ch-3 sp: 460 ch-3 sps.
Rnd 3: Ch 1, (sc in last ch-3 sp made, work Picot) twice, ★ (sc in next ch-3 sp, work Picot) across to next corner ch-3 sp, (sc, work Picot) twice in corner ch-3 sp; repeat from ★ 2 times **more**, (sc in next ch-3 sp, work Picot) across; join with slip st to first sc, finish off.

Pretty in Pink

This light-and-airy wrap is pretty in pink — or whatever color you choose! Crocheted in a hue that complements your décor, the afghan will breathe new life into a room.

Finished Size: 47" x 66"

MATERIALS
Worsted Weight Yarn:
   31 ounces, (880 grams, 2,020 yards)
Crochet hook, size J (6.00 mm) **or** size needed
   for gauge

GAUGE: In pattern, one repeat = 5^1/$_4$";
          6 rows = 4^1/$_4$"

Gauge Swatch: 6^1/$_2$"w x 4^1/$_4$"h
Ch 28.
Work same as Afghan Body for 6 rows.
Finish off.

STITCH GUIDE

FRONT POST DOUBLE CROCHET
   (abbreviated FPdc)
YO, insert hook from **front** to **back** around post of st indicated *(Fig. 10, page 139)*, YO and pull up a loop (3 loops on hook), (YO and draw through 2 loops on hook) twice.
BACK POST DOUBLE CROCHET
   (abbreviated BPdc)
YO, insert hook from **back** to **front** around post of st indicated *(Fig. 10, page 139)*, YO and pull up a loop (3 loops on hook), (YO and draw through 2 loops on hook) twice.
DECREASE
Pull up a loop in next 2 sps, YO and draw through all 3 loops on hook.
PICOT
Ch 5, sc in third ch from hook, ch 2.

AFGHAN BODY

Ch 128, place marker in fourth ch from hook for st placement.
Row 1: Dc in sixth ch from hook, ch 1, ★ skip next 3 chs, (2 dc, ch 2) twice in next ch, skip next 5 chs, (dc, ch 2) twice in next ch, skip next 5 chs, (2 dc, ch 2, 2 dc) in next ch, ch 1, skip next 3 chs, dc in next ch, ch 1; repeat from ★ across to last 2 chs, skip next ch, dc in last ch: 68 sts and 44 sps.

Row 2 (Right side)**:** Ch 4 **(counts as first dc plus ch 1, now and throughout)**, turn; work FPdc around next dc, ch 1, ★ skip next ch-1 sp, (2 dc, ch 2, 2 dc) in next ch-2 sp, skip next ch-2 sp, 7 dc in next ch-2 sp, skip next ch-2 sp, (2 dc, ch 2, 2 dc) in next ch-2 sp, ch 1, skip next ch-1 sp, work FPdc around next dc, ch 1; repeat from ★ 5 times **more**, skip next ch, dc in next ch: 99 sts and 26 sps.
Row 3: Ch 4, turn; work BPdc around next FPdc, ch 1, ★ skip next ch-1 sp, (2 dc, ch 2) twice in next ch-2 sp, (dc, ch 2) twice in center dc of next 7-dc group, (2 dc, ch 2, 2 dc) in next ch-2 sp, ch 1, skip next ch-1 sp, work BPdc around next FPdc, ch 1; repeat from ★ across to last ch-1 sp, skip last ch-1 sp, dc in last dc: 69 sts and 44 sps.
Row 4: Ch 4, turn; work FPdc around next BPdc, ch 1, ★ skip next ch-1 sp, (2 dc, ch 2, 2 dc) in next ch-2 sp, skip next ch-2 sp, 7 dc in next ch-2 sp, skip next ch-2 sp, (2 dc, ch 2, 2 dc) in next ch-2 sp, ch 1, skip next ch-1 sp, work FPdc around next BPdc, ch 1; repeat from ★ across to last ch-1 sp, skip last ch-1 sp, dc in last dc: 99 sts and 26 sps.
Rows 5-73: Repeat Rows 3 and 4, 34 times; then repeat Row 3 once **more**; do **not** finish off.

EDGING

Rnd 1: Ch 5 **(counts as first dc plus ch 2)**, turn; work FPdc around next BPdc, ch 2, ★ skip next ch-1 sp, (dc, ch 3, dc) in next ch-2 sp, ch 1, skip next ch-2 sp, 7 dc in next ch-2 sp, ch 1, skip next ch-2 sp, (dc, ch 3, dc) in next ch-2 sp, ch 2, skip next ch-1 sp, work FPdc around next BPdc, ch 2; repeat from ★ across to last ch-1 sp, skip last ch-1 sp, (dc, ch 3, dc) in last dc, ch 2; working across end of rows, dc in first row, ch 2, † skip next row, (dc, ch 3, dc) in next row, ch 1, skip next row, 7 dc in next row, ch 1, skip next row, (dc, ch 3, dc) in next row, ch 2, skip next row, dc in next row, ch 2 †; repeat from † to † across to marked ch, (dc, ch 3, dc) in marked ch, ch 2; working in free loops of beginning ch *(Fig. 17b, page 141)* and around posts of dc on Row 1, work FPdc around next dc, ch 2, ♥ skip next 3 chs, (dc, ch 3, dc) in next ch, ch 1, skip next 5 chs, 7 dc in next ch, ch 1, skip next 5 chs, (dc, ch 3, dc) in next ch, ch 2, skip next 3 chs, work FPdc around next dc, ch 2 ♥; repeat from ♥ to ♥ across to last 2 chs, skip

next ch, (dc, ch 3, dc) in last ch, ch 2; working across end of rows, dc in first row, ch 2, repeat from † to † across, dc in same st as first dc, ch 1, hdc in first dc to form last ch-3 sp: 30 7-dc groups and 192 sps.

Rnd 2: Ch 6 **(counts as first dc plus ch 3, now and throughout)**, turn; dc in last ch-3 sp made, ★ † ch 2, skip next ch-2 sp, work BPdc around next st, ch 2, skip next ch-2 sp, [(dc, ch 3) twice in next ch-3 sp, (dc, ch 2, dc) in center dc of next 7-dc group, ch 3, skip next ch-1 sp, (dc, ch 3, dc) in next ch-3 sp, ch 2, skip next ch-2 sp, work BPdc around next st, ch 2, skip next ch-2 sp] across to next corner ch-3 sp †, [dc, (ch 3, dc) 3 times] in corner ch-3 sp; repeat from ★ 2 times **more**, then repeat from † to † once, (dc, ch 3, dc) in same sp as first dc, ch 1, hdc in first dc to form last ch-3 sp: 230 sps.

Rnd 3: Ch 3 **(counts as first dc, now and throughout)**, turn; 3 dc in last ch-3 sp made, ★ † ch 3, dc in next ch-3 sp, ch 2, skip next ch-2 sp, work FPdc around next BPdc, ch 2, [skip next ch-2 sp, (dc, ch 3, dc) in next ch-3 sp, ch 1, skip next ch-3 sp, 7 dc in next ch-2 sp, ch 1, skip next ch-3 sp, (dc, ch 3, dc) in next ch-3 sp, ch 2, skip next ch-2 sp, work FPdc around next BPdc, ch 2] across to within 2 sps of next corner ch-3 sp, skip next ch-2 sp, dc in next ch-3 sp, ch 3 †, 7 dc in corner ch-3 sp; repeat from ★ 2 times **more**, then repeat from † to † once, 3 dc in same sp as first dc; join with slip st to first dc: 34 7-dc groups and 196 sps.

Continued on page 60.

Rnd 4: Ch 6, turn; ★ † (dc, ch 3, dc) in next ch-3 sp, ch 2, skip next ch-2 sp, work BPdc around next FPdc, ch 2, skip next ch-2 sp, (dc, ch 3) twice in next ch-3 sp, [(dc, ch 2, dc) in center dc of next 7-dc group, ch 3, skip next ch-1 sp, (dc, ch 3, dc) in next ch-3 sp, ch 2, skip next ch-2 sp, work BPdc around next FPdc, ch 2, skip next ch-2 sp, (dc, ch 3) twice in next ch-3 sp] across to next corner 7-dc group †, (dc, ch 3) twice in center dc of corner 7-dc group; repeat from ★ 2 times **more**, then repeat from † to † once, dc in same st as first dc, ch 1, hdc in first dc to form last ch-3 sp: 238 sps.

Rnd 5: Ch 3, turn; 3 dc in last ch-3 sp made, ★ † ch 2, dc in next ch-3 sp, ch 2, (dc, ch 3, dc) in next ch-3 sp, ch 2, skip next ch-2 sp, work FPdc around next BPdc, ch 2, skip next ch-2 sp, (dc, ch 3, dc) in next ch-3 sp, [ch 1, skip next ch-3 sp, 7 dc in next ch-2 sp, ch 1, skip next ch-3 sp, (dc, ch 3, dc) in next ch-3 sp, ch 2, skip next ch-2 sp, work FPdc around next BPdc, ch 2, skip next ch-2 sp, (dc, ch 3, dc) in next ch-3 sp] across to within one ch-3 sp of next corner ch-3 sp, ch 2, dc in next ch-3 sp, ch 2 †, 7 dc in corner ch-3 sp; repeat from ★ 2 times **more**, then repeat from † to † once, 3 dc in same sp as first dc; join with slip st to first dc: 34 7-dc groups and 212 sps.

Rnd 6: Ch 6, turn; ★ † dc in next ch-2 sp, ch 1, work BPdc around next dc, ch 2, skip next ch-2 sp, (dc, ch 3, dc) in next ch-3 sp, ch 2, skip next ch-2 sp, work BPdc around next FPdc, ch 2, [skip next ch-2 sp, (dc, ch 3) twice in next ch-3 sp, (dc, ch 2, dc) in center dc of next 7-dc group, ch 3, skip next ch-1 sp, (dc, ch 3, dc) in next ch-3 sp, ch 2, skip next ch-2 sp, work BPdc around next FPdc, ch 2] across to within 4 sps of next corner 7-dc group, skip next ch-2 sp, (dc, ch 3, dc) in next ch-3 sp, ch 2, skip next ch-2 sp, work BPdc around next dc, ch 1, dc in next ch-2 sp, ch 3 †, (dc, ch 3) twice in center dc of corner 7-dc group; repeat from ★ 2 times **more**, then repeat from † to † once, dc in same st as first dc, ch 1, hdc in first dc to form last ch-3 sp: 254 sps.

Rnd 7: Ch 3, turn; 3 dc in last ch-3 sp made, ★ † ch 3, dc in next ch-3 sp, [ch 2, skip next sp, work FPdc around next BPdc, ch 2, skip next ch-2 sp, (dc, ch 3, dc) in next ch-3 sp] twice, [ch 1, skip next ch-3 sp, 7 dc in next ch-2 sp, ch 1, skip next ch-3 sp, (dc, ch 3, dc) in next ch-3 sp, ch 2, skip next ch-2 sp, work FPdc around next BPdc, ch 2, skip next ch-2 sp, (dc, ch 3, dc) in next ch-3 sp] across to within 3 sps of next corner ch-3 sp, ch 2, skip next ch-2 sp, work FPdc around next BPdc, ch 2, skip next ch-1 sp, dc in next ch-3 sp, ch 3 †, 7 dc in corner ch-3 sp; repeat from ★ 2 times **more**, then repeat from † to † once, 3 dc in same sp as first dc; join with slip st to first dc: 34 7-dc groups and 220 sps.

Rnd 8: Ch 6, turn; ★ † (dc, ch 3, dc) in next ch-3 sp, [ch 2, skip next ch-2 sp, work BPdc around next FPdc, ch 2, skip next ch-2 sp, (dc, ch 3, dc) in next ch-3 sp] twice, [ch 3, (dc, ch 2, dc) in center dc of next 7-dc group, ch 3, skip next ch-1 sp, (dc, ch 3, dc) in next ch-3 sp, ch 2, skip next ch-2 sp, work BPdc around next FPdc, ch 2, skip next ch-2 sp, (dc, ch 3, dc) in next ch-3 sp] across to within 3 sps of next corner 7-dc group, ch 2, skip next ch-2 sp, work BPdc around next FPdc, ch 2, skip next ch-2 sp, (dc, ch 3) twice in next ch-3 sp †, (dc, ch 3) twice in center dc of corner 7-dc group; repeat from ★ 2 times **more**, then repeat from † to † once, dc in same st as first dc, ch 2, sc in first dc to form last ch-3 sp: 262 sps.

Rnd 9: Ch 3, turn; dc in last ch-3 sp made, ★ † ch 3, skip next ch-3 sp, (dc, ch 3, dc) in next ch-3 sp, [ch 2, skip next ch-2 sp, work FPdc around next BPdc, ch 2, skip next ch-2 sp, (dc, ch 3, dc) in next ch-3 sp] twice, [ch 1, skip next ch-3 sp, 7 dc in next ch-2 sp, ch 1, skip next ch-3 sp, (dc, ch 3, dc) in next ch-3 sp, ch 2, skip next ch-2 sp, work FPdc around next BPdc, ch 2, skip next ch-2 sp, (dc, ch 3, dc) in next ch-3 sp] across to within 4 sps of next corner ch-3 sp, ch 2, skip next ch-2 sp, work FPdc around next BPdc, ch 2, skip next ch-2 sp, (dc, ch 3) twice in next ch-3 sp, skip next ch-3 sp †, 7 dc in corner ch-3 sp; repeat from ★ 2 times **more**, then repeat from † to † once, 5 dc in same sp as first dc; join with slip st to first dc: 34 7-dc groups and 228 sps.

Rnd 10: Ch 1, do **not** turn; sc in same st, ch 5, ★ † (sc in next ch-3 sp, ch 5) twice, (decrease, ch 5, sc in next ch-3 sp, ch 5) twice, [skip next ch-1 sp and next dc, sc in next dc, ch 5, skip next 3 dc, sc in next dc, ch 5, skip next ch-1 sp, sc in next ch-3 sp, ch 5, decrease, ch 5, sc in next ch-3 sp, ch 5] across to within 4 sps of next corner 7-dc group, decrease, ch 5, (sc in next ch-3 sp, ch 5) twice, skip next dc, sc in next dc †, ch 5, skip next 3 dc, sc in next dc, ch 5; repeat from ★ 2 times **more**, then repeat from † to † once, ch 2, dc in first sc to form last ch-5 sp: 194 ch-5 sps.

Rnd 11: Ch 1, sc in last ch-5 sp made, work Picot, ★ † (sc in next ch-5 sp, work Picot) 4 times, decrease, work Picot, [(sc in next ch-5 sp, work Picot) 3 times, decrease, work Picot] across to within 4 ch-5 sps of next corner ch-5 sp, (sc in next ch-5 sp, work Picot) 4 times †, (sc, work Picot) twice in corner ch-5 sp; repeat from ★ 2 times **more**, then repeat from † to † once, sc in same sp as first sc, work Picot; join with slip st to first sc, finish off.

Vibrant Visions

This cover-up is bursting with gorgeous hues that are sure to attract the eye, as well as lots of compliments! The vibrant pattern is made up of squares.

Finished Size: 55" x 74$^1/_2$"

MATERIALS
Worsted Weight Yarn:
Purple - 24$^1/_2$ ounces, (700 grams, 1,385 yards)
Ecru - 16 ounces, (450 grams, 905 yards)
Lt Purple - 12$^1/_2$ ounces, (350 grams, 710 yards)
Green - 10$^1/_2$ ounces, (300 grams, 595 yards)
Crochet hook, size I (5.50 mm) **or** size needed for gauge
Yarn needle

GAUGE: Each Square = 14"
Each Strip = 18" wide

Gauge Swatch: 5$^1/_4$" diameter
(at widest point across Center)
Work same as Square A through Rnd 4.

SQUARE A (Make 8)
With Ecru, ch 3 **loosely**.
Rnd 1 (Right side): 11 Hdc in third ch from hook; join with slip st to top of beginning ch-3, finish off: 12 sts.
Note: Loop a short piece of yarn around any stitch to mark Rnd 1 as **right** side.
Rnd 2: With **right** side facing, join Green with slip st in same st as joining; ch 3, place marker in last ch made for st placement, (dc, ch 3, slip st) in same st, ch 2, skip next 2 hdc, ★ (slip st, ch 3, dc, ch 3, slip st) in next hdc, ch 2, skip next 2 hdc; repeat from ★ 2 times **more**; join with slip st to joining slip st, finish off: 4 dc.
Rnd 3: With **right** side facing, join Purple with slip st in marked ch; ch 3, remove marker and place in last ch made for st placement, ★ † 3 dc in next dc, ch 3, slip st in next ch, ch 3, skip next 2 chs and next slip st, slip st in next ch-2 sp, ch 3, skip next slip st and next 2 chs †, slip st in next ch, ch 3; repeat from ★ 2 times **more**, then repeat from † to † once; join with slip st to joining slip st, finish off: 12 dc.

Rnd 4: With **right** side facing, join Lt Purple with slip st in marked ch; ch 3, remove marker and place in last ch made for st placement, ★ † dc in next dc, 3 dc in next dc, dc in next dc, ch 3, slip st in next ch, ch 3, skip next 2 chs and next slip st, slip st in next ch, skip next 2 chs, dc in Back Loop Only of next slip st *(Fig. 16, page 141)*, skip next 2 chs, slip st in next ch, ch 3, skip next slip st and next 2 chs †, slip st in next ch, ch 3, working in **both** loops; repeat from ★ 2 times **more**, then repeat from † to † once; join with slip st to joining slip st, finish off: 24 dc.
Rnd 5: With **right** side facing, join Ecru with slip st in marked ch; ch 3, remove marker and place in last ch made for st placement, ★ † dc in next 2 dc, 3 dc in next dc, dc in next 2 dc, ch 3, slip st in next ch, ch 3, skip next 2 chs and next slip st, slip st in next ch, skip next 2 chs and next slip st, 3 dc in Back Loop Only of next dc †, (skip next slip st and next 2 chs, slip st in next ch, ch 3) twice, working in **both** loops; repeat from ★ 2 times **more**, then repeat from † to † once, skip next slip st and next 2 chs, slip st in next ch, ch 3, skip next slip st and next 2 chs; join with slip st to joining slip st, finish off: 40 dc.
Rnd 6: With **right** side facing, join Purple with slip st in marked ch; ch 3, remove marker and place in last ch made for st placement, ★ † dc in next 3 dc, 3 tr in next dc, dc in next 3 dc, ch 3, slip st in next ch, ch 3, skip next 2 chs and next slip st, slip st in next ch, skip next 2 chs and next slip st, dc in next dc, 3 dc in next dc, dc in next dc †, (skip next slip st and next 2 chs, slip st in next ch, ch 3) twice; repeat from ★ 2 times **more**, then repeat from † to † once, skip next slip st and next 2 chs, slip st in next ch, ch 3, skip next slip st and next 2 chs; join with slip st to joining slip st, finish off: 44 dc and 12 tr.
Rnd 7: With **right** side facing, join Lt Purple with sc in marked ch *(see Joining With Sc, page 140)*; sc in next 3 dc, ★ † hdc in next tr, 5 hdc in next tr, hdc in next tr, sc in next 4 sts, ch 3, skip next 2 chs and next slip st, slip st in next ch, skip next 2 chs and next slip st, 2 dc in next dc, dc in next 3 dc, 2 dc in next dc, skip next slip st and next 2 chs, slip st in next ch, ch 3, skip next slip st and next 2 chs †, sc in next 4 sts; repeat from ★ 2 times **more**, then repeat from † to † once; join with slip st to first sc, finish off: 28 dc, 28 hdc, and 32 sc.

Continued on page 62.

Rnd 8: With **right** side facing, join Green with sc in center hdc of any corner 5-hdc group; (hdc, sc) in same st, ★ † sc in next 8 sts, skip next 2 chs and next slip st, dc in next 7 dc, skip next slip st and next 2 chs, sc in next 8 sts †, (sc, hdc, sc) in next hdc; repeat from ★ 2 times **more**, then repeat from † to † once; join with slip st to first sc, finish off: 104 sts.

Rnd 9: With **right** side facing, join Purple with slip st in center hdc of any corner 3-st group; ★ † ch 5, dc in fourth ch from hook and in last ch **(Block made)**, skip next sc, (slip st in next st, slip st in Back Loop Only of next 3 sts, slip st in **both** loops of next st, ch 5, dc in fourth ch from hook and in last ch, skip next st) 4 times †, slip st in next hdc; repeat from ★ 2 times **more**, then repeat from † to † once; join with slip st to first slip st, finish off: 20 Blocks.

Rnd 10: With **right** side facing, join Ecru with slip st in Back Loop Only of same st as joining; ch 4 **(counts as first tr, now and throughout)**, (tr, dtr, 2 tr) in same st, ★ † skip next 2 chs, sc in next 3 chs, (skip next 2 dc and next slip st, tr in Back Loop Only of next 3 slip sts, skip next slip st and next 2 chs, sc in next 3 chs) across to within 2 dc of next corner slip st, skip next 2 dc †, (2 tr, dtr, 2 tr) in Back Loop Only of corner slip st; repeat from ★ 2 times **more**, then repeat from † to † once; join with slip st to first tr, finish off: 128 sts.

Rnd 11: With **right** side facing, join Purple with slip st in center dtr of any corner 5-st group; ★ † ch 5, dc in fourth ch from hook and in last ch, skip next tr, (slip st in next tr, slip in Back Loop Only of next 3 sc, slip st in **both** loops of next tr, ch 5, dc in fourth ch from hook and in last ch, skip next tr) across to center dtr of next corner 5-st group †, slip st in center dtr; repeat from ★ 2 times **more**, then repeat from † to † once; join with slip st to first slip st, finish off: 24 Blocks.

Rnd 12: With Lt Purple, repeat Rnd 10: 152 sts.

Rnd 13: Repeat Rnd 11: 28 Blocks.

Rnd 14: Repeat Rnd 10: 176 sts.

SQUARE B (Make 7)

Make same as Square A through Rnd 11: 24 Blocks.

Rnd 12: With Green, repeat Rnd 10: 128 sts.

Rnd 13: Repeat Rnd 11: 28 Blocks.

Rnd 14: Repeat Rnd 10: 176 sts.

SQUARE ASSEMBLY

With Ecru, using Placement Diagram as a guide, and working through **both** loops, whipstitch Squares together *(Fig. 21b, page 142)*, forming 3 vertical strips of 5 Squares each, beginning in center dtr of first corner 5-st group and ending in center dtr of next corner 5-st group.

PLACEMENT DIAGRAM

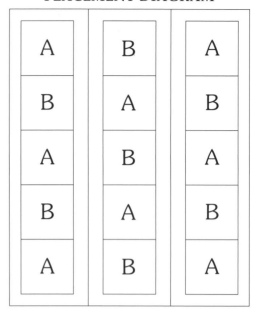

STRIP BORDER

Rnd 1: With **right** side facing and working across short edge of Strip, join Purple with slip st in center dtr of first corner 5-st group; † ch 5, dc in fourth ch from hook and in last ch, skip next tr, (slip st in next tr, slip st in Back Loop Only of next 3 sc, slip st in **both** loops of next tr, ch 5, dc in fourth ch from hook and in last ch, skip next tr) 7 times, slip st in next dtr, ch 5, dc in fourth ch from hook and in last ch, skip next tr, (slip st in next tr, slip st in Back Loop Only of next 3 sc, slip st in **both** loops of next tr, ch 5, dc in fourth ch from hook and in last ch, skip next tr) 7 times, ★ slip st in same st as joining on same Square and in same st as joining on next Square, ch 5, place marker in third ch from hook for st placement, dc in fourth ch from hook and in last ch, skip next tr, (slip st in next tr, slip st in Back Loop Only of next 3 sc, slip st in **both** loops of next tr, ch 5, dc in fourth ch from hook and in last ch, skip next tr) 7 times; repeat from ★ across to center dtr of next corner 5-st group †, slip st in center dtr, repeat from † to † once; join with slip st to first slip st, finish off: 96 Blocks.

Rnd 2: With **right** side facing, join Green with slip st in Back Loop Only of same st as joining; ch 4, (tr, dtr, 2 tr) in same st, † skip next 2 chs, sc in next 3 chs, (skip next 2 dc and next slip st, tr in Back Loop Only in next 3 slip sts, skip next slip st and next 2 chs, sc in next 3 chs) 7 times, skip next 2 dc, (2 tr, dtr, 2 tr) in Back Loop Only of next slip st, skip next 2 chs, sc in next 3 chs, (skip next 2 dc and next slip st, tr in Back Loop Only of next 3 slip sts, skip next slip st and next 2 chs, sc in next 3 chs) 7 times, ★ sc in next marked ch and next 2 chs, (skip next 2 dc and next

slip st, tr in Back Loop Only of next 3 slip sts, skip next slip st and next 2 chs, sc in next 3 chs) 7 times; repeat from ★ across to within 2 dc of next corner slip st, skip next 2 dc †, (2 tr, dtr, 2 tr) in Back Loop Only of corner slip st, repeat from † to † once; join with slip st to first tr, finish off: 560 sts.

Rnd 3: With **right** side facing, join Purple with slip st in center dtr of first group; † ch 5, dc in fourth ch from hook and in last ch, skip next tr, (slip st in next tr, slip st in Back Loop Only of next 3 sc, slip st in **both** loops of next tr, ch 5, dc in fourth ch from hook and in last ch, skip next tr) 8 times, slip st in next dtr, ch 5, dc in fourth ch from hook and in last ch, skip next tr, slip st in next tr, (slip st in Back Loop Only of next 3 sc, slip st in **both** loops of next tr, ch 5, dc in fourth ch from hook and in last ch, skip

next tr, slip st in next tr) 7 times, slip st in Back Loop Only of next 6 sc, slip st in **both** loops of next tr, ch 5, dc in fourth ch from hook and in last ch, skip next tr, ★ (slip st in next tr, slip st in Back Loop Only of next 3 sc, slip st in **both** loops of next tr, ch 5, dc in fourth ch from hook and in last ch, skip next tr) 6 times, slip st in next tr, slip st in Back Loop Only of next 6 sc, slip st in **both** loops of next tr, ch 5, dc in fourth ch from hook and in last ch, skip next tr; repeat from ★ 2 times **more**, (slip st in next tr, slip st in Back Loop Only of next 3 sc, slip st in **both** loops of next tr, ch 5, dc in fourth ch from hook and in last ch, skip next tr) 7 times †, slip st in next dtr, repeat from † to † once; join with slip st to first slip st, finish off: 92 Blocks.

Continued on page 64.

Rnd 4: With **right** side facing, join Lt Purple with slip st in Back Loop Only of same st as joining; ch 4, (tr, dtr, 2 tr) in same st, † skip next 2 chs, sc in next 3 chs, (skip next 2 dc and next slip st, tr in Back Loop Only of next 3 slip sts, skip next slip st and next 2 chs, sc in next 3 chs) 8 times, skip next 2 dc, (2 tr, dtr, 2 tr) in Back Loop Only of next slip st, skip next 2 chs, sc in next 3 chs, (skip next 2 dc and next slip st, tr in Back Loop Only of next 3 slip sts, skip next slip st and next 2 chs, sc in next 3 chs) 7 times, skip next 2 dc and next slip st, tr in Back Loop Only of next 6 slip sts, skip next slip st and next 2 chs, sc in next 3 chs, ★ (skip next 2 dc and next slip st, tr in Back Loop Only of next 3 slip sts, skip next slip st and next 2 chs, sc in next 3 chs) 6 times, skip next 2 dc and next slip st, tr in Back Loop Only of next 6 slip sts, skip next slip st and next 2 chs, sc in next 3 chs; repeat from ★ 2 times **more**, (skip next 2 dc and next slip st, tr in Back Loop Only of next 3 slip sts, skip next slip st and next 2 chs, sc in next 3 chs) 7 times †, skip next 2 dc, (2 tr, dtr, 2 tr) in Back Loop Only of next slip st, repeat from † to † once; join with slip st to first tr, finish off: 584 sts. Repeat on remaining 2 strips.

STRIP ASSEMBLY

With Lt Purple, using Placement Diagram as a guide, page 62, and working through **both** loops, whipstitch strips together beginning in center dtr of first corner 5-st group and ending in center dtr of next corner 5-st group.

EDGING

With **wrong** side facing, join Ecru with slip st in center dtr of any corner 5-st group; dc in next st, (slip st in next st, dc in next st) around; join with slip st to first slip st, finish off.

Carnival

Flowing with generous fringe, this cover-up is a carnival of colors! Variegated yarn, finely contrasted with black, creates a look that is sure to draw admiring glances.

Finished Size: 48" x 64"

MATERIALS
Worsted Weight Yarn:
Variegated - 22 ounces, (620 grams, 1,330 yards)
Black - 21$^1/_2$ ounces, (610 grams, 1,410 yards)
Crochet hook, size I (5.50 mm) **or** size needed for gauge

GAUGE: In pattern,
(dc, ch 1, dc) 3 times = 2$^1/_2$";
6 rows = 3$^1/_2$"

Gauge Swatch: 4$^3/_4$"w x 4$^1/_4$"h
With Black, ch 19.
Work same as Afghan Body for 7 rows.

Note: Each row is worked across length of Afghan. When joining yarn and finishing off, leave an 8" length to be worked into fringe.

AFGHAN BODY

With Black, ch 235, place marker in third ch from hook for st placement.

Row 1 (Right side)**:** (Dc, ch 1, dc) in fifth ch from hook, ★ skip next 2 chs, (dc, ch 1, dc) in next ch; repeat from ★ across to last 2 chs, skip next ch, dc in last ch; finish off: 77 ch-1 sps.
Note: Loop a short piece of yarn around any stitch to mark Row 1 as **right** side.

Row 2: With **wrong** side facing, join Variegated with slip st in first dc; ch 3 **(counts as first dc, now and throughout)**, (dc, ch 1, dc) in each ch-1 sp across to last dc, skip last dc, dc in next ch; finish off.

Row 3: With **right** side facing, join Black with slip st in first dc; ch 3, (dc, ch 1, dc) in each ch-1 sp across to last 2 dc, skip next dc, dc in last dc; finish off.

Row 4: With **wrong** side facing, join Variegated with slip st in first dc; ch 3, (dc, ch 1, dc) in each ch-1 sp across to last 2 dc, skip next dc, dc in last dc; finish off.

Repeat Rows 3 and 4 until Afghan Body measures approximately 47" from beginning ch, ending by working Row 3.

TRIM
FIRST SIDE
Row 1: With **wrong** side facing, join Black with sc in first dc on last row *(see Joining With Sc, page 140)*; sc in next dc, ★ ch 1, skip next ch-1 sp, sc in next 2 dc; repeat from ★ across; finish off.

Row 2: With **right** side facing, join Black with slip st in first sc; ch 2, skip next sc, slip st in next ch-1 sp, ch 2, ★ skip next 2 sc, slip st in next ch-1 sp, ch 2; repeat from ★ across to last 2 sc, skip next sc, slip st in last sc; finish off.

SECOND SIDE
Row 1: With **wrong** side facing and working in free loops of beginning ch *(Fig. 17b, page 141)*, join Black with sc in marked ch; sc in next ch, ★ ch 1, skip next ch, sc in next 2 chs; repeat from ★ across; finish off.

Row 2: With **right** side facing, join Black with slip st in first sc; ch 2, skip next sc, slip st in next ch-1 sp, ch 2, ★ skip next 2 sc, slip st in next ch-1 sp, ch 2; repeat from ★ across to last 2 sc, skip next sc, slip st in last sc; finish off.

Holding 4 strands of each color yarn together, each 17" long, add additional fringe in every other row across short edges of Afghan *(Figs. 22b & d, page 142)*.

Rosy Comfort

*"Take time to smell the roses" simply means to slow down and enjoy life's little pleasures.
So why not while away the hours wrapped in the comfort of this rosy afghan?*

Finished Size: 50^1/$_2$" x 69"

MATERIALS
Worsted Weight Yarn:
64 ounces, (1,820 grams, 3,615 yards)
Crochet hook, size J (6.00 mm) **or** size needed for gauge

GAUGE: In pattern, 11 sts and 8 rows = 4"

STITCH GUIDE

FRONT POST DOUBLE CROCHET
(abbreviated FPdc)
YO, insert hook from **front** to **back** around post of st indicated *(Fig. 10, page 139)*, YO and pull up a loop (3 loops on hook), (YO and draw through 2 loops on hook) twice. Skip st behind FPdc.

BACK POST DOUBLE CROCHET
(abbreviated BPdc)
YO, insert hook from **back** to **front** around post of FPdc indicated *(Fig. 10, page 139)*, YO and pull up a loop (3 loops on hook), (YO and draw through 2 loops on hook) twice. Skip FPdc behind BPdc.

POPCORN
4 Dc in dc indicated, drop loop from hook, insert hook in first dc of 4-dc group, hook dropped loop and draw through st *(Fig. 14, page 140)*.

PICOT
Ch 3, sc in third ch from hook.

AFGHAN BODY
Ch 138 **loosely**, place marker in third ch from hook for st placement.
Row 1: Dc in fourth ch from hook **(3 skipped chs count as first dc)** and in each ch across: 136 dc.
Row 2 (Right side): Ch 3 **(counts as first dc, now and throughout)**, turn; dc in next dc, ✝ work FPdc around next dc, dc in next dc, work Popcorn in next dc, dc in next dc, (work FPdc around next dc, dc in next dc) 3 times, work Popcorn in next dc, dc in next dc, work FPdc around next dc ✝, ★ dc in next 4 dc, repeat from ✝ to ✝ once; repeat from ★ across to last 2 dc, dc in last 2 dc: 40 FPdc and 16 Popcorn.

Row 3: Ch 3, turn; dc in next dc, ✝ work BPdc around next FPdc, dc in next 3 sts, work BPdc around next FPdc, (dc in next dc, work BPdc around next FPdc) twice, dc in next 3 sts, work BPdc around next FPdc ✝, ★ dc in next 4 dc, repeat from ✝ to ✝ once; repeat from ★ across to last 2 dc, dc in last 2 dc: 40 BPdc.
Row 4: Ch 3, turn; dc in next dc, ✝ work FPdc around next BPdc, dc in next dc, work Popcorn in next dc, dc in next dc, (work FPdc around next BPdc, dc in next dc) 3 times, work Popcorn in next dc, dc in next dc, work FPdc around next BPdc ✝, ★ dc in next 4 dc, repeat from ✝ to ✝ once; repeat from ★ across to last 2 dc, dc in last 2 dc: 40 FPdc and 16 Popcorn.
Repeat Rows 3 and 4 until Cover-up measures approximately 66^1/$_2$" from beginning ch, ending by working Row 3; do **not** finish off.

EDGING
Rnd 1: Ch 3, turn; dc in same st, work 137 dc evenly spaced across to last dc, 3 dc in last dc; work 200 dc evenly spaced across end of rows; working in free loops of beginning ch *(Fig. 17b, page 141)*, 3 dc in marked ch, work 137 dc evenly spaced across to last ch, 3 dc in last ch; work 200 dc evenly spaced across end of rows, dc in same st as first dc; join with slip st to first dc: 686 dc.
Rnd 2: Ch 1, turn; sc in same st, work Picot, ★ (sc in next dc, work Picot, skip next 2 dc) across to next corner 3-dc group, (sc in next dc, work Picot) 3 times, skip next 2 dc; repeat from ★ 2 times **more**, sc in next dc, work Picot, (skip next 2 dc, sc in next dc, work Picot) across; join with slip st to first sc, finish off.

Dazzling Dahlias

This bed of dazzling dahlias is abloom with lush color! Worked holding two strands of yarn together, the afghan takes shape quickly.

Finished Size: 47" x 62"

MATERIALS

Worsted Weight Yarn:
Green - 29 ounces, (820 grams, 1,640 yards)
Variegated - 22 ounces, (620 grams, 1,275 yards)
Pink - 14^1/$_2$ ounces, (410 grams, 785 yards)
Crochet hook, size Q (15.00 mm) **or** size needed for gauge

Note: Afghan is worked holding two strands of yarn together.

GAUGE: Each Square = 7"

Gauge Swatch: 3^3/$_4$" square
Work same as Square through Rnd 1.

STITCH GUIDE

BEGINNING CLUSTER
Ch 2, ★ YO, insert hook in sp indicated, YO and pull up a loop, YO and draw through 2 loops on hook; repeat from ★ once **more**, YO and draw through all 3 loops on hook *(Figs. 11a & b, page 139)*.
CLUSTER (uses one sp)
★ YO, insert hook in sp indicated, YO and pull up a loop, YO and draw through 2 loops on hook; repeat from ★ 2 times **more**, YO and draw through all 4 loops on hook *(Figs. 11a & b, page 139)*.

SQUARE (Make 48)

With Pink, ch 4; join with slip st to form a ring.
Rnd 1 (Right side): Work Beginning Cluster in ring, ch 1, (work Cluster in ring, ch 1) 7 times; join with slip st to top of Beginning Cluster, finish off: 8 Clusters and 8 ch-1 sps.
Note: Loop a short piece of yarn around any stitch to mark Rnd 1 as **right** side.

Rnd 2: With **right** side facing, join Variegated with slip st in any ch-1 sp; work (Beginning Cluster, ch 1, Cluster) in same sp, work (Cluster, ch 1, Cluster) in each ch-1 sp around; join with slip st to top of Beginning Cluster, finish off: 16 Clusters and 8 ch-1 sps.
Rnd 3: With **right** side facing, join Green with slip st in any ch-1 sp; work (Beginning Cluster, ch 1, Cluster) in same sp, ★ † skip next Cluster, (dc, hdc) in next Cluster, sc in next ch-1 sp, skip next Cluster, (hdc, dc) in next Cluster †, work (Cluster, ch 1, Cluster) in next ch-1 sp; repeat from ★ 2 times **more**, then repeat from † to † once; join with slip st to top of Beginning Cluster, finish off: 20 sts, 8 Clusters, and 4 ch-1 sps.

ASSEMBLY

Join Squares as follows:
With **right** side of first Square facing and working in Back Loops Only *(Fig. 16, page 141)*, join Green with slip st in any corner ch-1; holding second Square with **right** side facing, slip st in corresponding corner ch-1, ★ slip st in next st on **first Square**, slip st in next st on **second Square**; repeat from ★ across to next corner ch-1 on **both** Squares, slip st in corner ch-1 on **first Square**, slip st in corner ch-1 on **second Square**; finish off.
Join remaining Squares together, forming 6 vertical strips of 8 Squares each; then join strips together in same manner, working in joinings.

EDGING

With **right** side facing and working in Back Loops Only, join Green with slip st in any corner ch-1; ch 1, ★ † (slip st in next st, ch 1) 7 times, [slip st in next joining, ch 1, (slip st in next st, ch 1) 7 times] across to next corner ch-1 †, slip st in corner ch-1, ch 1; repeat from ★ 2 times **more**, then repeat from † to † once; join with slip st to first slip st, finish off.

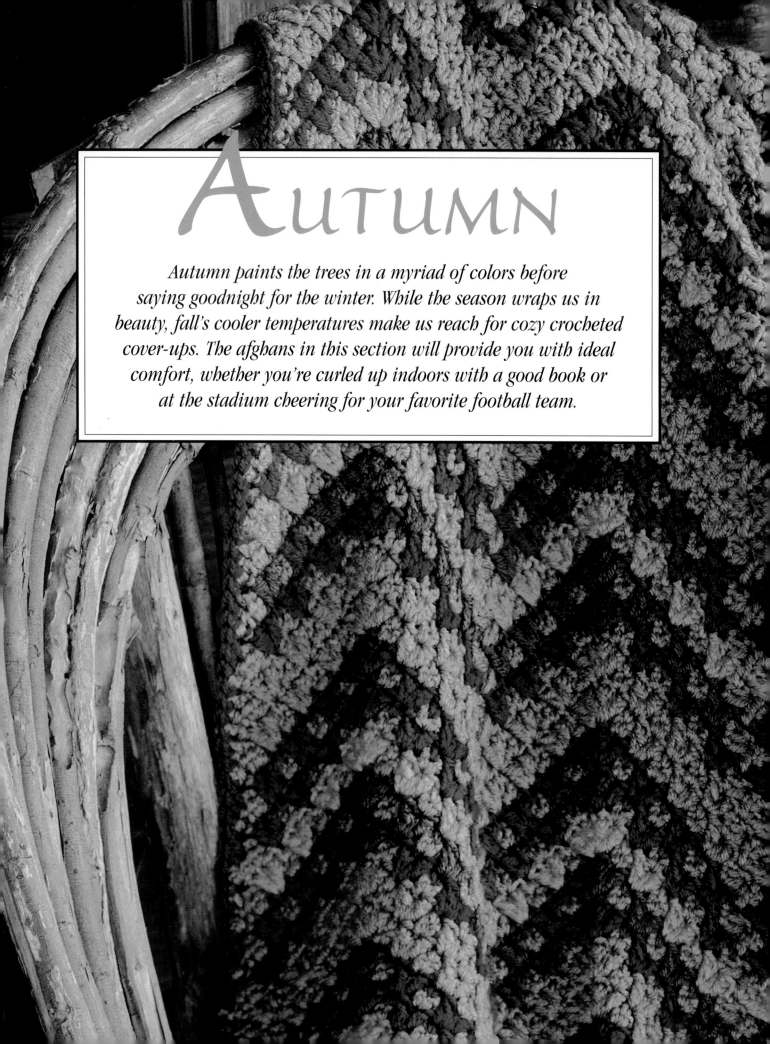

AUTUMN

Autumn paints the trees in a myriad of colors before saying goodnight for the winter. While the season wraps us in beauty, fall's cooler temperatures make us reach for cozy crocheted cover-ups. The afghans in this section will provide you with ideal comfort, whether you're curled up indoors with a good book or at the stadium cheering for your favorite football team.

Harvest Blend

*Crocheted in a blend of fall hues, this fringed afghan reflects the bounty of harvesttime.
The colorful stripes are accentuated with toasty brown webbing.*

Finished Size: 45$\frac{1}{2}$" x 60"

MATERIALS
Worsted Weight Yarn:
Brown - 18 ounces, (510 grams, 1,235 yards)
Green - 11 ounces, (310 grams, 755 yards)
Yellow - 9$\frac{1}{2}$ ounces, (270 grams, 650 yards)
Red - 9$\frac{1}{2}$ ounces, (270 grams, 650 yards)
Crochet hook, size H (5.00 mm) **or** size needed for gauge

GAUGE: In pattern, (sc, 5 dc) 3 times = 3$\frac{3}{4}$"
8 rows = 4"

Gauge Swatch: 4" square
Ch 14 **loosely**.
Work same as Afghan for 8 rows.

Note: Each row is worked across length of Afghan. When joining yarn and finishing off, leave an 8" length to be worked into fringe.

AFGHAN
With Green, ch 194 **loosely**.
Row 1 (Right side): Sc in back ridge of second ch from hook *(Fig. 2b, page 137)* and each ch across; finish off: 193 sc.
Note: Loop a short piece of yarn around any stitch to mark Row 1 as **right** side.
Row 2: With **wrong** side facing, join Brown with slip st in first sc; ch 3 **(counts as first dc)**, ★ skip next sc, (dc, ch 1, dc) in next sc, skip next sc, dc in next sc; repeat from ★ across; finish off: 145 dc and 48 ch-1 sps.
Row 3: With **right** side facing, join Yellow with sc in first dc *(see Joining With Sc, page 140)*; ★ 5 dc in next ch-1 sp, skip next dc, sc in next dc; repeat from ★ across; finish off: 48 5-dc groups and 49 sc.

Row 4: With **wrong** side facing, join Brown with slip st in first sc; ch 4 **(counts as first tr, now and throughout)**, ★ skip next 2 dc, (dc, ch 1, dc) in next dc, skip next 2 dc, tr in next sc; repeat from ★ across; finish off: 145 sts and 48 ch-1 sps.
Row 5: With **right** side facing, join Red with sc in first tr; ★ 5 dc in next ch-1 sp, skip next dc, sc in next tr; repeat from ★ across; finish off: 48 5-dc groups and 49 sc.
Row 6: With **wrong** side facing, join Brown with slip st in first sc; ch 4, ★ skip next 2 dc, (dc, ch 1, dc) in next dc, skip next 2 dc, tr in next sc; repeat from ★ across; finish off: 145 sts and 48 ch-1 sps.
Row 7: With **right** side facing, join Green with sc in first tr; ★ 5 dc in next ch-1 sp, skip next dc, sc in next tr; repeat from ★ across; finish off: 48 5-dc groups and 49 sc.
Row 8: With **wrong** side facing, join Brown with slip st in first sc; ch 4, ★ skip next 2 dc, (dc, ch 1, dc) in next dc, skip next 2 dc, tr in next sc; repeat from ★ across; finish off: 145 sts and 48 ch-1 sps.
Row 9: With **right** side facing, join Yellow with sc in first tr; ★ 5 dc in next ch-1 sp, skip next dc, sc in next tr; repeat from ★ across; finish off: 48 5-dc groups and 49 sc.
Rows 10-90: Repeat Rows 4-9, 13 times; then repeat Rows 4-6 once **more**.
Row 91: With **right** side facing, join Green with sc in first tr; sc in next dc and in each ch-1 sp and each st across; finish off.

Holding 4 strands of Brown and 4 strands of corresponding color yarn together, each 17" long, add additional fringe in every other row across short edges of Afghan *(Figs. 22b & d, page 142)*.

Thanksgiving

Radiating fall's golden splendor, this hearty cover-up exudes a sense of warmth. Front and back post treble crochet stitches create a comfy texture for which you'll be thankful on cool evenings.

Finished Size: 48" x 68"

MATERIALS
Worsted Weight Yarn:
   64 ounces, (1,820 grams, 3,615 yards)
Crochet hook, size I (5.50 mm) **or** size needed for gauge

GAUGE: In pattern, one repeat = 2³/₄";
   5 rows = 3"

Gauge Swatch: 7"w x 3"h
Ch 33.
Work same as Afghan for 5 rows.
Finish off.

STITCH GUIDE

> **BACK POST TREBLE CROCHET**
>   *(abbreviated BPtr)*
> YO twice, insert hook from **back** to **front** around post of st indicated *(Fig. 10, page 139)*, YO and pull up a loop (4 loops on hook), (YO and draw through 2 loops on hook) 3 times.
>
> **FRONT POST TREBLE CROCHET**
>   *(abbreviated FPtr)*
> YO twice, insert hook from **front** to **back** around post of st indicated *(Fig. 10, page 139)*, YO and pull up a loop (4 loops on hook), (YO and draw through 2 loops on hook) 3 times.

AFGHAN
Ch 213.
Row 1 (Right side): Dc in fourth ch from hook **(3 skipped chs count as first dc)** and in next 4 chs, ch 1, skip next 3 chs, (3 dc, ch 3, 3 dc) in next ch, ch 1, ★ skip next 3 chs, dc in next 5 chs, ch 1, skip next 3 chs, (3 dc, ch 3, 3 dc) in next ch, ch 1; repeat from ★ across to last 9 chs, skip next 3 chs, dc in last 6 chs: 194 dc and 51 sps.

Row 2: Ch 3 **(counts as first dc, now and throughout)**, turn; work BPtr around next dc, (dc in next dc, work BPtr around next dc) twice, ch 3, skip next ch-1 sp and next 3 dc, sc in next ch-3 sp, ch 3, ★ skip next 3 dc and next ch-1 sp, work BPtr around next dc, (dc in next dc, work BPtr around next dc) twice, ch 3, skip next ch-1 sp and next 3 dc, sc in next ch-3 sp, ch 3; repeat from ★ across to last 9 dc, skip next 3 dc and next ch-1 sp, (work BPtr around next dc, dc in next dc) 3 times: 109 sts and 34 ch-3 sps.

Row 3: Ch 3, turn; ★ work FPtr around next BPtr, (dc in next dc, work FPtr around next BPtr) twice, ch 1, skip next ch-3 sp, (3 dc, ch 3, 3 dc) in next sc, ch 1; repeat from ★ across to last 6 sts, (work FPtr around next BPtr, dc in next dc) 3 times: 194 sts and 51 sps.

Row 4: Ch 3, turn; work BPtr around next FPtr, (dc in next dc, work BPtr around next FPtr) twice, ch 3, skip next ch-1 sp and next 3 dc, sc in next ch-3 sp, ch 3, ★ skip next 3 dc and next ch-1 sp, work BPtr around next FPtr, (dc in next dc, work BPtr around next FPtr) twice, ch 3, skip next ch-1 sp and next 3 dc, sc in next ch-3 sp, ch 3; repeat from ★ across to last 9 sts, skip next 3 dc and next ch-1 sp, (work BPtr around next FPtr, dc in next dc) 3 times: 109 sts and 34 ch-3 sps.

Repeat Rows 3 and 4 until Afghan measures approximately 68" from beginning ch, ending by working a **wrong** side row.
Finish off.

Holding 7 strands of yarn together, each 20" long, add fringe evenly across short edges of Afghan *(Figs. 22a & c, page 142)*.

Spiced Tea

Spice up your fall décor with a robust blanket! The welcoming wrap is worked in mile-a-minute strips and then whipstitched together for lasting comfort.

Finished Size: 50" x 69"

MATERIALS
Worsted Weight Yarn:
- Peach - 37 ounces, (1,050 grams, 2,430 yards)
- Rust - 27 ounces, (770 grams, 1,775 yards)
- Crochet hook, size H (5.00 mm) **or** size needed for gauge
- Yarn needle

GAUGE: Each Strip = 5" wide

Gauge Swatch: $2^1/8$"w x $3^3/4$"h
Work same as Center for 5 rows.
Finish off.

STITCH GUIDE

> **FRONT POST DOUBLE CROCHET**
> **(abbreviated FPdc)**
> YO, insert hook from **front** to **back** around post of st indicated **(Fig. 10, page 139)**, YO and pull up a loop (3 loops on hook), (YO and draw through 2 loops on hook) twice.
>
> **FRONT POST TREBLE CROCHET**
> **(abbreviated FPtr)**
> YO twice, insert hook from **front** to **back** around post of st indicated **(Fig. 10, page 139)**, YO and pull up a loop (4 loops on hook), (YO and draw through 2 loops on hook) 3 times.

STRIP (Make 10)
CENTER
Row 1 (Right side): With Peach, ch 4, 6 dc in fourth ch from hook **(3 skipped chs count as first dc)**: 7 dc.
Note: Loop a short piece of yarn around any stitch to mark Row 1 as **right** side and bottom edge.
Row 2: Ch 3 **(counts as first dc, now and throughout)**, do **not** turn; 7 dc in free loop of same ch **(Fig. 17b, page 141)**, dc in first dc on Row 1: 9 dc.
Rows 3-92: Ch 3, turn; skip next 3 dc, 7 dc in next dc, skip next 3 dc, dc in last dc.
Finish off.

BORDER
Rnd 1: With **right** side facing and working in end of rows, join Rust with slip st in Row 2; ch 3, dc in same row, tr around **top** of dc on same row **(Fig. 1)**, 2 dc in next row, ★ tr around top of dc on same row, 2 dc in next row; repeat from ★ across to next 7-dc group; 2 dc in each of next 7 dc; working in end of rows, 2 dc in first row, (tr around top of first dc on next row, 2 dc in same row) across to last 7-dc group, 2 dc in each of last 7 dc; join with slip st to first dc, finish off: 572 sts.

Fig. 1

Rnd 2: With **right** side facing, join Peach with sc in same st as joining **(see Joining With Sc, page 140)**; sc in Back Loop Only of next dc **(Fig. 16, page 141)**, † work FPtr around next tr, (sc in Back Loop Only of next 2 dc, work FPtr around next tr) 89 times †, sc in Back Loop Only of next 18 dc, repeat from † to † once, sc in Back Loop Only of last 16 dc; join with slip st to Back Loop Only of first sc.
Rnd 3: Ch 1, sc in Back Loop Only of same st and next sc, † work FPtr around next FPtr, (sc in Back Loop Only of next 2 sc, work FPtr around next FPtr) 89 times, (sc in Back Loop Only of next sc, 2 sc in Back Loop Only of next sc) 8 times †, sc in Back Loop Only of next 2 sc, repeat from † to † once; join with slip st to **both** loops of first sc, finish off: 588 sts.

TRIM
FIRST SIDE
With **right** side facing, join Rust with sc in Back Loop Only of same st as joining; sc in Back Loop Only of next sc, (work FPdc around next FPtr, sc in Back Loop Only of next 2 sc) 90 times, leave remaining sts unworked; finish off.

Continued on page 78.

SECOND SIDE

With **right** side facing, skip next 22 sc from last sc worked and join Rust with sc in Back Loop Only of next sc; sc in Back Loop Only of next sc, (work FPdc around next FPtr, sc in Back Loop Only of next 2 sc) 90 times, leave remaining sts unworked; finish off.

ASSEMBLY

With Rust and working through inside loops only, whipstitch Strips together **(Fig. 21a, page 142)**, beginning in first sc of Trim and ending in last sc of Trim.

Rock-A-Bye Blanket

Baby will love being snuggled in this downy-soft coverlet. The rippled design is crocheted holding two strands of worsted weight yarn together, working in back loops only to create the plush texture.

Finished Size: 36" x 51"

MATERIALS
Worsted Weight Yarn:
  White - 26 ounces, (740 grams, 1,470 yards)
  Blue - 10$^1/_2$ ounces, (300 grams, 595 yards)
  Pink - 5$^1/_2$ ounces, (160 grams, 310 yards)
Crochet hook, size P (10.00 mm) **or** size needed for gauge

Note: Afghan is worked holding two strands of yarn together.

GAUGE: In pattern, 2 repeats = 4$^1/_4$";
  6 rows = 3$^1/_4$"

Gauge Swatch: 4$^1/_2$"w x 3$^1/_2$"h
Ch 13 **loosely**.
Work same as Afghan for 6 rows.
Finish off.

To work **color change**, work the last sc to within one step of completion, cut one strand of yarn, hook new yarn and remaining strand and draw through both loops on hook **(Fig. 19, page 141)**.

AFGHAN

With one strand of White and one strand of Blue, ch 118 **loosely**.
Row 1: Working in back ridges of beginning ch **(Fig. 2b, page 137)**, sc in second ch from hook and in next ch, 3 sc in next ch, sc in next 2 chs, ★ skip next 2 chs, sc in next 2 chs, 3 sc in next ch, sc in next 2 chs; repeat from ★ across: 119 sc.

Row 2 (Right side): Ch 1, turn; sc in first sc, skip next sc, working in Back Loops Only **(Fig. 16, page 141)**, sc in next sc, 3 sc in next sc, ★ sc in next 2 sc, skip next 2 sc, sc in next 2 sc, 3 sc in next sc; repeat from ★ across to last 3 sc, sc in next sc, skip next sc, sc in **both** loops of last sc changing to one strand of White and one strand of Pink.
Row 3: Ch 1, turn; sc in both loops of first sc, skip next sc, working in Back Loops Only, sc in next sc, 3 sc in next sc, ★ sc in next 2 sc, skip next 2 sc, sc in next 2 sc, 3 sc in next sc; repeat from ★ across to last 3 sc, sc in next sc, skip next sc, sc in **both** loops of last sc.
Row 4: Ch 1, turn; sc in both loops of first sc, skip next sc, working in Back Loops Only, sc in next sc, 3 sc in next sc, ★ sc in next 2 sc, skip next 2 sc, sc in next 2 sc, 3 sc in next sc; repeat from ★ across to last 3 sc, sc in next sc, skip next sc, sc in **both** loops of last sc changing to one strand of White and one strand of Blue.
Rows 5 and 6: Repeat Rows 3 and 4 changing to two strands of White at end of last row.
Rows 7 and 8: Repeat Rows 3 and 4.
Rows 9 and 10: Repeat Rows 3 and 4 changing to one strand of White and one strand of Pink at end of last row.
Rows 11-93: Repeat Rows 3-10, 10 times; then repeat Rows 3-5 once **more**.
Row 94: Ch 1, turn; sc in both loops of first sc, skip next sc, working in Back Loops Only, sc in next sc, 3 sc in next sc, ★ sc in next 2 sc, skip next 2 sc, sc in next 2 sc, 3 sc in next sc; repeat from ★ across to last 3 sc, sc in next sc, skip next sc, sc in **both** loops of last sc; finish off.

Log Cabin Legacy

This eye-catching throw offers the comforts of home, even from the porch of a cabin in the woods. Long double crochet stitches enhance the afghan's appeal.

Finished Size: 46¹/₂" x 63¹/₂"

MATERIALS

Worsted Weight Yarn:
  Black - 25 ounces, (710 grams, 1,720 yards)
  Tan - 13 ounces, (370 grams, 895 yards)
  Burgundy - 12¹/₂ ounces, (360 grams, 860 yards)
Crochet hook, size H (5.00 mm) **or** size needed for gauge

GAUGE: In pattern, 14 sts = 4"; 2 repeats = 3¹/₂"; 14 rows = 5"

Gauge Swatch: 8¹/₂"w x 5"h
Ch 32 **loosely**.
Work same as Afghan for 14 rows.

STITCH GUIDE

LONG DOUBLE CROCHET
  (abbreviated LDC)
YO, insert hook in st or sp indicated, YO and pull up a loop even with last st made (3 loops on hook), (YO and draw through 2 loops on hook) twice *(Fig. 9, page 139)*.

AFGHAN

With Black, ch 164 **loosely**.
Row 1: Sc in second ch from hook and in next ch, ★ ch 3, skip next 3 chs, sc in next 9 chs; repeat from ★ across to last 5 chs, ch 3, skip next 3 chs, sc in last 2 chs: 121 sc and 14 ch-3 sps.
Row 2 (Right side): Ch 3 **(counts as first dc, now and throughout)**, turn; dc in next sc, ch 3, (dc in next 9 sc, ch 3) across to last 2 sc, dc in last 2 sc; finish off.
Note: Loop a short piece of yarn around any stitch to mark Row 2 as **right** side.

Row 3: With **wrong** side facing, join Tan with sc in first dc *(see Joining With Sc, page 140)*; sc in next dc, working around previous row *(Fig. 18, page 141)*, work 3 LDC in ch-3 sp one row **below** next ch-3, ★ sc in next 3 dc, ch 3, skip next 3 dc, sc in next 3 dc, working around previous row, work 3 LDC in ch-3 sp one row **below** next ch-3; repeat from ★ across to last 2 dc, sc in last 2 dc; do **not** finish off: 124 sts and 13 ch-3 sps.
Row 4: Ch 3, turn; dc in next 7 sts, ★ ch 3, skip next ch-3 sp, dc in next 9 sts; repeat from ★ across to last ch-3 sp, ch 3, skip last ch-3 sp, dc in last 8 sts; finish off.
Row 5: With **wrong** side facing, join Burgundy with sc in first dc; sc in next dc, ★ ch 3, skip next 3 dc, sc in next 3 dc, working around previous 2 rows, work LDC in each of 3 skipped dc 2 rows **below** next ch-3, sc in next 3 dc; repeat from ★ across to last 5 dc, ch 3, skip next 3 dc, sc in last 2 dc; do **not** finish off: 121 sts and 14 ch-3 sps.
Row 6: Ch 3, turn; dc in next sc, ★ ch 3, skip next ch-3 sp, dc in next 9 sts; repeat from ★ across to last ch-3 sp, ch 3, skip last ch-3 sp, dc in last 2 sc; finish off.
Row 7: With **wrong** side facing, join Tan with sc in first dc; sc in next dc, working around previous 2 rows, work LDC in each of 3 skipped dc 2 rows **below** next ch-3, ★ sc in next 3 dc, ch 3, skip next 3 dc, sc in next 3 dc, working around previous 2 rows, work LDC in each of 3 skipped dc 2 rows **below** next ch-3; repeat from ★ across to last 2 dc, sc in last 2 dc; do not finish off: 124 sts and 13 ch-3 sps.
Row 8: Ch 3, turn; dc in next 7 sts, ★ ch 3, skip next ch-3 sp, dc in next 9 sts; repeat from ★ across to last ch-3 sp, ch 3, skip last ch-3 sp, dc in last 8 sts; finish off.
Rows 9 and 10: With Black, repeat Rows 5 and 6; do **not** finish off: 121 sts and 14 ch-3 sps.
Row 11: Ch 1, turn; sc in first 2 dc, working around previous 2 rows, work LDC in each of 3 skipped dc 2 rows **below** next ch-3, ★ sc in next 3 dc, ch 3, skip next 3 dc, sc in next 3 dc, working around previous 2 rows, work LDC in each of 3 skipped dc 2 rows **below** next ch-3; repeat from ★ across to last 2 dc, sc in last 2 dc; do **not** finish off: 124 sts and 13 ch-3 sps.

Row 12: Repeat Row 4; do **not** finish off.
Row 13: Ch 1, turn; sc in first 2 dc, ★ ch 3, skip next 3 dc, sc in next 3 dc, working around previous 2 rows, work LDC in each of 3 skipped dc 2 rows **below** next ch-3, sc in next 3 dc; repeat from ★ across to last 5 dc, ch 3, skip next 3 dc, sc in last 2 dc; do **not** finish off: 121 sts and 14 ch-3 sps.
Row 14: Repeat Row 6.
Rows 15 and 16: With Burgundy, repeat Rows 7 and 8.
Rows 17 and 18: With Tan, repeat Rows 5 and 6.
Rows 19 and 20: With Burgundy, repeat Rows 7 and 8.
Rows 21 and 22: With Black, repeat Rows 5 and 6; do **not** finish off: 121 sts and 14 ch-3 sps.
Row 23: Repeat Row 11.

Row 24: Repeat Row 4; do **not** finish off.
Row 25: Repeat Row 13.
Row 26: Repeat Row 16.
Rows 27 and 28: Repeat Rows 7 and 8.
Rows 29-176: Repeat Rows 5-28, 6 times; then repeat Rows 5-8 once **more**.
Row 177: With **wrong** side facing, join Black with sc in first dc; sc in next 7 dc, working around previous 2 rows, work LDC in each of 3 skipped dc 2 rows **below** next ch-3, ★ sc in next 9 dc, working around previous 2 rows, work LDC in each of 3 skipped dc 2 rows **below** next ch-3; repeat from ★ across to last 8 dc, sc in last 8 dc; do **not** finish off: 163 sts.
Row 178: Ch 3, turn; dc in next sc and in each st across; finish off.

Home on the Range

Featuring a bold Southwestern design, this blanket will make you feel right at home on any range. Chains of fringe complete the rugged look.

Finished Size: 46" x 60½"

MATERIALS

Worsted Weight Yarn:
- Ecru - 19½ ounces, (550 grams, 1,335 yards)
- Brown - 16¾ ounces, (470 grams, 1,150 yards)
- Red - 5¼ ounces, (150 grams, 360 yards)
- Yellow - 5¼ ounces, (150 grams, 360 yards)

Crochet hook, size I (5.50 mm) **or** size needed for gauge

GAUGE: In pattern, 13 sts and 12 rows = 4"

Gauge Swatch: 4" square
Ch 14 **loosely**.
Row 1: Sc in second ch from hook and in each ch across: 13 sc.
Rows 2-12: Ch 1, turn; sc in each sc across.
Finish off.

Note: Each row is worked across length of Afghan.

AFGHAN BODY

With Brown, ch 197 **loosely**; finish off.
Row 1 (Right side): With Brown, ch 16 **loosely (fringe made)**, sc in each ch across beginning ch-197, ch 16 **loosely (fringe made)**; finish off: 197 sc.
Note: Loop a short piece of yarn around any stitch to mark Row 1 as **right** side.
All rows are worked with **right** side facing throughout.
Row 2: With Brown, ch 16 **loosely**, sc in first sc, sc in Back Loop Only of each sc across to last sc (*Fig. 16, page 141*), sc in **both** loops of last sc, ch 16 **loosely**; finish off.
Row 3: With Red, ch 16 **loosely**, sc in both loops of first sc, sc in Back Loop Only of each st across to last sc, sc in **both** loops of last sc, ch 16 **loosely**; finish off.
Row 4: With Red, ch 16 **loosely**, sc in both loops of first sc, dc in free loop of sc one row **below** next sc (*Fig. 17a, page 141*), skip sc behind dc, ★ sc in Back Loop Only of next sc, dc in free loop of sc one row **below** next sc, skip sc behind dc; repeat from ★ across to last sc, sc in **both** loops of last sc, ch 16 **loosely**; finish off: 98 dc and 99 sc.

Row 5: With Yellow, ch 16 **loosely**, sc in both loops of first sc, sc in Back Loop Only of each st across to last sc, sc in **both** loops of last sc, ch 16 **loosely**; finish off: 197 sc.
Row 6: With Yellow, ch 16 **loosely**, sc in both loops of first sc, sc in Back Loop Only of next sc, ★ dc in free loop of sc one row **below** next sc, skip sc behind dc, sc in Back Loop Only of next sc; repeat from ★ across to last sc, sc in **both** loops of last sc, ch 16 **loosely**; finish off: 97 dc and 100 sc.
Rows 7 and 8: With Ecru, repeat Rows 3 and 4.
Row 9: With Brown, ch 16 **loosely**, sc in both loops of first sc, sc in Back Loop Only of each st across to last sc, sc in **both** loops of last sc, ch 16 **loosely**; finish off: 197 sc.
Row 10: With Ecru, ch 16 **loosely**, sc in both loops of first sc, sc in Back Loop Only of each st across to last sc, sc in **both** loops of last sc, ch 16 **loosely**; finish off.
Row 11: Repeat Row 9.
Row 12: With Ecru, ch 16 **loosely**, sc in both loops of first sc, (dc in free loop of st one row **below** next sc) twice, skip 2 sc behind dc, sc in Back Loop Only of next st, (dc in free loop of st one row **below** next sc) 3 times, skip 3 sc behind dc, [sc in Back Loop Only of next 2 sts, (dc in free loop of st one row **below** next sc) 3 times, skip 3 sc behind dc] twice, ★ sc in Back Loop Only of next 3 sts, (dc in free loop of st one row **below** next sc) 3 times, skip 3 sc behind dc, [sc in Back Loop Only of next 2 sts, (dc in free loop of st one row **below** next sc) 3 times, skip 3 sc behind dc] twice; repeat from ★ across to last 4 sts, sc in Back Loop Only of next st, (dc in free loop of st one row **below** next sc) twice, sc in **both** loops of last sc, ch 16 **loosely**; finish off: 112 dc and 85 sc.

Continued on page 84.

Row 13: With Brown, ch 16 **loosely**, sc in both loops of first sc, sc in Back Loop Only of next 2 dc, dc in free loop of sc one row **below** next sc, skip sc behind dc, sc in Back Loop Only of next 3 sts, [(dc in free loop of sc one row **below** next sc) twice, skip 2 sc behind dc, sc in Back Loop Only of next 3 sts] twice, dc in free loop of sc one row **below** next sc, skip sc behind dc, ★ sc in Back Loop Only of next st, dc in free loop of sc one row **below** next sc, skip sc behind dc, sc in Back Loop Only of next 3 sts, [(dc in free loop of sc one row **below** next sc) twice, skip 2 sc behind dc, sc in Back Loop Only of next 3 sts] twice, dc in free loop of sc one row **below** next sc, skip sc behind dc; repeat from ★ across to last 3 sts, sc in Back Loop Only of next 2 dc, sc in **both** loops of last sc, ch 16 **loosely**; finish off: 72 dc and 125 sc.

Row 14: With Ecru, ch 16 **loosely**, sc in both loops of first sc, (dc in free loop of dc one row **below** next sc) twice, skip 2 sc behind dc, sc in Back Loop Only of next 3 sts, ★ dc in free loop of st one row **below** next sc, skip sc behind dc, sc in Back Loop Only of next 3 sts; repeat from ★ across to last 3 sts, (dc in free loop of dc one row **below** next sc) twice, skip 2 sc behind dc, sc in **both** loops of last sc, ch 16 **loosely**; finish off: 51 dc and 146 sc.

Row 15: With Brown, ch 16 **loosely**, sc in both loops of first sc, sc in Back Loop Only of next 4 sts, dc in free loop of sc one row **below** next sc, skip sc behind dc, sc in Back Loop Only of next 3 sts, dc in free loop of sc one row **below** next sc, skip sc behind dc, sc in Back Loop Only of next st, dc in free loop of sc one row **below** next sc, skip sc behind dc, sc in Back Loop Only of next 3 sts, dc in free loop of sc one row **below** next sc, skip sc behind dc, ★ sc in Back Loop Only of next 5 sts, dc in free loop of sc one row **below** next sc, skip sc behind dc, sc in Back Loop Only of next 3 sts, dc in free loop of sc one row **below** next sc, skip sc behind dc, sc in Back Loop Only of next st, dc in free loop of sc one row **below** next sc, skip sc behind dc, sc in Back Loop Only of next 3 sts, dc in free loop of sc one row **below** next sc, skip sc behind dc; repeat from ★ across to last 5 sts, sc in Back Loop Only of next 4 sts, sc in **both** loops of last sc, ch 16 **loosely**; finish off: 48 dc and 149 sc.

Row 16: With Ecru, ch 16 **loosely**, sc in both loops of first sc, (dc in free loop of dc one row **below** next sc) twice, skip 2 sc behind dc, sc in Back Loop Only of next st, dc in free loop of sc one row **below** next sc, skip sc behind dc, ★ sc in Back Loop Only of next 3 sts, dc in free loop of sc one row **below** next sc, skip sc behind dc; repeat from ★ across to last 4 sts, sc in Back Loop Only of next st, (dc in free loop of dc one row **below** next sc) twice, skip 2 sc behind dc, sc in **both** loops of last sc, ch 16 **loosely**; finish off: 52 dc and 145 sc.

Row 17: With Brown, ch 16 **loosely**, sc in both loops of first sc, sc in Back Loop Only of next 2 dc, dc in free loop of sc one row **below** next sc, skip sc behind dc, sc in Back Loop Only of next 3 sts, dc in free loop of sc one row **below** next sc, skip sc behind dc, sc in Back Loop Only of next 5 sts, dc in free loop of sc one row **below** next sc, skip sc behind dc, sc in Back Loop Only of next 3 sts, dc in free loop of sc one row **below** next sc, skip sc behind dc, ★ sc in Back Loop Only of next st, dc in free loop of sc one row **below** next sc, skip sc behind dc, sc in Back Loop Only of next 3 sts, dc in free loop of sc one row **below** next sc, skip sc behind dc, sc in Back Loop Only of next 5 sts, dc in free loop of sc one row **below** next sc, skip sc behind dc, sc in Back Loop Only of next 3 sts, dc in free loop of sc one row **below** next sc, skip sc behind dc; repeat from ★ across to last 3 sts, sc in Back Loop Only of next 2 dc, sc in **both** loops of last sc, ch 16 **loosely**; finish off: 48 dc and 149 sc.

Rows 18-20: Repeat Rows 14 and 15 once, then repeat Row 14 once **more**.

Row 21: Repeat Row 17.

Row 22: Repeat Row 16.

Row 23: Repeat Row 15.

Row 24: Repeat Row 14.

Row 25: Repeat Row 13.

Row 26: Repeat Row 12.

Row 27: Repeat Row 9.

Rows 28 and 29: With Ecru, ch 16 **loosely**, sc in both loops of first sc, sc in Back Loop Only of each sc across to last sc, sc in **both** loops of last sc, ch 16 **loosely**; finish off: 197 sc.

Row 30: With Ecru, ch 16 **loosely**, sc in both loops of first sc, dc in free loop of sc one row **below** next sc, skip sc behind dc, ★ sc in Back Loop Only of next sc, dc in free loop of sc one row **below** next sc, skip sc behind dc; repeat from ★ across to last sc, sc in **both** loops of last sc, ch 16 **loosely**; finish off: 98 dc and 99 sc.

Rows 31 and 32: Repeat Rows 5 and 6.

Rows 33 and 34: Repeat Rows 3 and 4.

Rows 35 and 36: With Brown, repeat Rows 5 and 6.

Rows 37-138: Repeat Rows 3-36, 3 times.

Row 139: With Brown, ch 16 **loosely**, sc in both loops of each sc across, ch 16 **loosely**; finish off.

TRIM
FIRST SIDE
With Brown, ch 16 **loosely**, with **right** side facing and working in sc across Row 139, slip st **loosely** in each sc across, ch 16 **loosely**; finish off.

SECOND SIDE
With Brown, ch 16 **loosely**, with **right** side facing and working in free loops of beginning ch-197 *(Fig. 17b, page 141)*, slip st **loosely** in each ch across, ch 16 **loosely**; finish off.

Sun-Baked Tiles

Ripples of clusters on a striped background lend this cover-up the appearance of sun-baked tiles. Drape it over your favorite piece of furniture to instantly warm up the room's atmosphere.

Finished Size: 46" x 65"

MATERIALS
Worsted Weight Yarn:
Maroon - 26 ounces, (740 grams, 1,470 yards)
Dk Coral - 16 ounces, (450 grams, 905 yards)
Lt Coral - 14 ounces, (400 grams, 790 yards)
Crochet hook, size I (5.50 mm) **or** size needed for gauge

GAUGE: In pattern, (sc, ch 1) 6 times = $3^1/_4$";
10 rows = 3"

Gauge Swatch: 9"w x 3"h
With Maroon, ch 34.
Work same as Afghan Body for 10 rows.

STITCH GUIDE

CLUSTER (uses one ch)
Ch 3, YO, insert hook in third ch from hook, YO and pull up a loop, YO and draw through 2 loops on hook, YO, insert hook in same ch, YO and pull up a loop, YO and draw through 2 loops on hook, YO and draw through all 3 loops on hook *(Figs. 11a& b, page 139)*.

Note: Each row is worked across length of Afghan. When joining yarn and finishing off, leave an 8" end to be worked into fringe.

AFGHAN BODY
With Maroon, ch 242.

Row 1 (Right side): Sc in second ch from hook, ★ ch 1, skip next ch, sc in next ch; repeat from ★ across; finish off: 121 sc and 120 chs.

Note: Loop a short piece of yarn around any stitch to mark Row 1 as **right** side.

Row 2: With **wrong** side facing, join Dk Coral with sc in first sc *(see Joining With Sc, page 140)*; (ch 1, skip next ch, sc in next st) 5 times, work Cluster, skip next sc, sc in next sc, ★ (ch 1, skip next ch, sc in next st) 6 times, work Cluster, skip next sc, sc in next sc; repeat from ★ across to last sc, ch 1, sc in last sc; finish off: 15 Clusters.

Row 3: With **right** side facing, join Maroon with sc in first sc; ch 1, sc in next sc, ch 1, working **behind** next Cluster *(Fig. 18, page 141)*, dc in skipped sc one row **below**, ★ ch 1, (sc in next sc, ch 1) 7 times, working **behind** next Cluster, dc in skipped sc one row **below**; repeat from ★ across to last 6 sc, (ch 1, sc in next sc) 6 times; finish off.

Continued on page 86.

Row 4: With **wrong** side facing, join Dk Coral with sc in first sc; ★ (ch 1, sc in next sc) 4 times, (work Cluster, skip next 3 sts, sc in next st) twice; repeat from ★ across; finish off: 30 Clusters.

Row 5: With **right** side facing, join Maroon with sc in first sc; ★ (ch 1, working **behind** next Cluster, dc in skipped sc one row **below**, ch 1, sc in next sc) twice, (ch 1, sc in next sc) 4 times; repeat from ★ across; finish off.

Row 6: With **wrong** side facing, join Dk Coral with sc in first sc; (ch 1, skip next ch, sc in next st) 5 times, work Cluster, skip next sc, sc in next dc, ★ (ch 1, skip next ch, sc in next st) 6 times, work Cluster, skip next sc, sc in next dc; repeat from ★ across to last sc, ch 1, sc in last sc; finish off: 15 Clusters.

Row 7: With **right** side facing, join Maroon with sc in first sc; ch 1, sc in next sc, ch 1, working **behind** next Cluster, dc in skipped sc one row **below**, ★ ch 1, (sc in next sc, ch 1) 7 times, working **behind** next Cluster, dc in skipped sc one row **below**; repeat from ★ across to last 6 sc, (ch 1, sc in next sc) 6 times; finish off.

Row 8: With **wrong** side facing, join Lt Coral with sc in first sc; (ch 1, skip next ch, sc in next st) 3 times, work Cluster, skip next 3 sts, sc in next st, ★ (ch 1, skip next ch, sc in next st) 6 times, work Cluster, skip next 3 sts, sc in next st; repeat from ★ across to last 6 sts, (ch 1, skip next ch, sc in next st) 3 times; finish off: 15 Clusters.

Row 9: With **right** side facing, join Maroon with sc in first sc; ch 1, (sc in next sc, ch 1) 3 times, working **behind** next Cluster, dc in skipped sc one row **below**, ★ ch 1, (sc in next sc, ch 1) 7 times, working **behind** next Cluster, dc in skipped sc one row **below**; repeat from ★ across to last 4 sc, (ch 1, sc in next sc) 4 times; finish off.

Row 10: With **wrong** side facing, join Lt Coral with sc in first sc; (ch 1, sc in next sc) twice, (work Cluster, skip next 3 sts, sc in next st) twice, ★ (ch 1, sc in next sc) 4 times, (work Cluster, skip next 3 sts, sc in next st) twice; repeat from ★ across to last 2 sc, (ch 1, sc in next sc) twice; finish off: 30 Clusters.

Row 11: With **right** side facing, join Maroon with sc in first sc; (ch 1, sc in next sc) twice, (ch 1, working **behind** next Cluster, dc in skipped sc one row **below**, ch 1, sc in next sc) twice, ★ (ch 1, sc in next sc) 4 times, (ch 1, working **behind** next Cluster, dc in skipped sc one row **below**, ch 1, sc in next sc) twice; repeat from ★ across to last 2 sc, (ch 1, sc in next sc) twice; finish off.

Rows 12 and 13: Repeat Rows 8 and 9.

Row 14: With **wrong** side facing, join Dk Coral with sc in first sc; ch 1, skip next ch, sc in next st, work Cluster, skip next 3 sts, sc in next st, ★ (ch 1, skip next ch, sc in next st) 6 times, work Cluster, skip next 3 sts, sc in next st; repeat from ★ across to last 10 sts, (ch 1, skip next ch, sc in next st) 5 times; finish off.

Row 15: With **right** side facing, join Maroon with sc in first sc; ch 1, (sc in next sc, ch 1) 5 times, working **behind** next Cluster, dc in skipped sc one row **below**, ★ ch 1, (sc in next sc, ch 1) 7 times, working **behind** next Cluster, dc in skipped sc one row **below**; repeat from ★ across to last 2 sc, (ch 1, sc in next sc) twice; finish off.

Row 16: With **wrong** side facing, join Dk Coral with sc in first sc; ★ (work Cluster, skip next 3 sts, sc in next st) twice, (ch 1, sc in next sc) 4 times; repeat from ★ across; finish off.

Row 17: With **right** side facing, join Maroon with sc in first sc; ★ (ch 1, sc in next sc) 4 times, (ch 1, working **behind** next Cluster, dc in skipped sc one row **below**, ch 1, sc in next sc) twice; repeat from ★ across; finish off.

Rows 18 and 19: Repeat Rows 14 and 15.

Rows 20-25: Repeat Rows 8-13.

Rows 26-151: Repeat Rows 2-25, 5 times; then repeat Rows 2-7 once **more**.

TRIM
FIRST SIDE

Row 1: With **wrong** side facing, join Maroon with sc in first sc on Row 151; ★ ch 1, skip next ch, sc in next st; repeat from ★ across; finish off.

Row 2: With **right** side facing, join Maroon with slip st in first sc; (slip st in next ch-1 sp, ch 1) across to last ch-1 sp, slip st in last ch-1 sp and in last sc; finish off.

SECOND SIDE

Row 1: With **right** side facing and working in free loops (*Fig. 17b, page 141*) and in sps across beginning ch, join Maroon with slip st in first ch; (slip st in next sp, ch 1) across to last sp, slip st in last sp and in next ch; finish off.

Holding 2 strands of corresponding color yarn together, each 17" long, add additional fringe in each row across short edges of Afghan (*Figs. 22b & d, page 142*).

Autumn Glory

Resembling a trail of fallen autumn leaves, ripples of rich color wind their way through this lap-of-luxury afghan. The thick throw would look nice in a den or study.

Finished Size: 46" x 64"

MATERIALS
Worsted Weight Yarn:
Tan - 26 ounces, (740 grams, 1,705 yards)
Purple - $10^1/2$ ounces, (300 grams, 690 yards)
Burgundy - 5 ounces, (140 grams, 330 yards)
Green - 5 ounces, (140 grams, 330 yards)
Gold - 5 ounces, (140 grams, 330 yards)
Crochet hook, size H (5.00 mm) **or** size needed for gauge

GAUGE: In pattern,
one repeat (point to point) = $6^1/2$";
10 rows = 4"

Gauge Swatch: 13"w x $6^3/4$"h
With Tan, ch 55 **loosely.**
Work same as Afghan Body for 10 rows.

STITCH GUIDE

BEGINNING DECREASE
Pull up a loop in same st and in next st, YO and draw through all 3 loops on hook **(counts as one sc).**
DECREASE
Pull up a loop in next 2 sts, YO and draw through all 3 loops on hook **(counts as one sc).**
CLUSTER
YO, insert hook in same st as last hdc made, YO and pull up a loop, ★ YO, skip **next** dc, insert hook in **next** sc, YO and pull up a loop; repeat from ★ once **more**, YO and draw through all 7 loops on hook **(Figs. 12a & b, page 139).**

AFGHAN BODY

With Tan, 185 **loosely.**
Row 1 (Wrong side): Hdc in second ch from hook and in next 2 chs, ★ † ch 1, skip next ch, (hdc in next 3 chs, ch 1, skip next ch) twice, (hdc, 2 dc) in next ch, ch 3, skip next ch, (2 dc, hdc) in next ch, ch 1, (skip next ch, hdc in next 3 chs, ch 1) twice †, skip next ch, hdc in next ch, (YO, insert hook in **next** ch, YO and pull up a loop) 3 times, YO and draw through all 7 loops on hook, hdc in next ch; repeat from ★

5 times **more**, then repeat from † to † once, skip next ch, hdc in next 2 chs, (YO, insert hook in **next** ch, YO and pull up a loop) twice, YO and draw through all 5 loops on hook; finish off: 150 sts and 49 sps.
Note: Loop a short piece of yarn around the **back** of any stitch on Row 1 to mark **right** side.
Row 2: With **right** side facing, join Purple with slip st in first st; ch 1, work beginning decrease, [working in **front** of Row 1 (*Fig. 18, page 141*), dc in next skipped ch on beginning ch, sc in next ch-1 sp on Row 1, working in **front** of Row 1, dc in same ch as last dc made, skip next hdc on Row 1, sc in next st] 3 times, ★ † working in **front** of Row 1, dc in next skipped ch on beginning ch, sc in next ch-3 sp on Row 1, working in **front** of Row 1, dc in same ch as last dc made, (sc in same sp as last sc made on Row 1, working in **front** of Row 1, dc in same ch as last dc made) twice, skip next dc on Row 1 †, sc in next dc, (working in **front** of Row 1, dc in next skipped ch on beginning ch, sc in next ch-1 sp on Row 1, working in **front** of Row 1, dc in same ch as last dc made, skip next hdc on Row 1, sc in next st) 6 times; repeat from ★ 5 times **more**, then repeat from † to † once, (sc in next st, working in **front** of Row 1, dc in next skipped ch on beginning ch, sc in next ch-1 sp on Row 1, working in **front** of Row 1, dc in same ch as last dc made, skip next hdc on Row 1) 3 times, decrease; finish off: 225 sts.
Row 3: With **wrong** side facing, join Tan with slip st in first sc; ch 1, work beginning decrease, 2 hdc in next sc, ★ † (ch 2, skip next 3 sts, 2 hdc in next sc) 3 times, ch 3, skip next 3 sts, (2 hdc in next sc, ch 2, skip next 3 sts) 3 times †, hdc in next sc, work Cluster, hdc in same st as last leg of Cluster just made; repeat from ★ 5 times **more**, then repeat from † to † once, 2 hdc in next sc, decrease; finish off: 108 sts and 49 sps.
Row 4: With **right** side facing, join Green with slip st in first sc; ch 1, work beginning decrease, ★ † [working in **front** of previous row, dc in skipped sc one row **below** next ch-2, sc in ch-2 sp, working in **front** of previous row, dc in same st as last dc made, skip next hdc, sc in sp **before** next hdc (*Fig. 20, page 141*)] 3 times, working in **front** of previous row, dc in skipped sc one row **below** next ch-3, sc in ch-3 sp, working in **front** of previous row,

dc in same st as last dc made, (sc in same sp as last sc made, working in **front** of previous row, dc in same st as last dc made) twice, (skip next hdc, sc in sp **before** next hdc, working in **front** of previous row, dc in skipped sc one row **below** next ch-2, sc in ch-2 sp, working in **front** of previous row, dc in same st as last dc made) 3 times, skip next hdc †, sc in next Cluster; repeat from ★ 5 times **more**, then repeat from † to † once, decrease; finish off: 225 sts.

Row 5: Repeat Row 3.
Row 6: With Gold, repeat Row 4.
Row 7: Repeat Row 3.
Row 8: With Burgundy, repeat Row 4.
Row 9: Repeat Row 3.
Row 10: With Purple, repeat Row 4.
Row 11: Repeat Row 3; do **not** finish off.

Row 12: Ch 1, turn; pull up a loop in first 2 sts, YO and draw through all 3 loops on hook, ★ † (working in **front** of previous row, dc in skipped sc one row **below** next ch-2, sc in ch-2 sp, working in **front** of previous row, dc in same st as last dc made, skip next hdc, sc in sp **before** next hdc) 3 times, working in **front** of previous row, dc in skipped sc one row **below** next ch-3, sc in ch-3 sp, working in **front** of previous row, dc in same st as last dc made, (sc in same sp as last sc made, working in **front** of previous row, dc in same st as last dc made) twice, (skip next hdc, sc in sp **before** next hdc, working in **front** of previous row, dc in skipped sc one row **below** next ch-2, sc in ch-2 sp, working in **front** of previous row, dc in same st as last dc made) 3 times, skip next hdc †, sc in next Cluster; repeat from ★ 5 times **more**, then repeat from † to † once, decrease: 225 sts.

Continued on page 90.

Row 13: Ch 1, turn; pull up a loop in first 2 sts, YO and draw through all 3 loops on hook, 2 hdc in next sc, ★ † (ch 2, skip next 3 sts, 2 hdc in next sc) 3 times, ch 3, skip next 3 sts, (2 hdc in next sc, ch 2, skip next 3 sts) 3 times †, hdc in next sc, work Cluster, hdc in same st as last leg of Cluster just made; repeat from ★ 5 times **more**, then repeat from † to † once, 2 hdc in next sc, decrease: 108 sts and 49 sps.
Rows 14 and 15: Repeat Rows 12 and 13. Finish off.
Row 16: With Purple, repeat Row 4.
Rows 17-150: Repeat Rows 3-16, 9 times; then repeat Rows 3-10 once **more**; at end of Row 150, do **not** finish off.

EDGING

Ch 1, do **not** turn; sc evenly across end of rows; working in free loops of beginning ch *(Fig. 17b, page 141)*, 3 sc in ch at base of first hdc, sc in next 11 chs, pull up a loop in next 3 chs, YO and draw through all 4 loops on hook, ★ sc in next 11 chs, 3 sc in next ch, sc in next 11 chs, pull up a loop in next 3 chs, YO and draw through all 4 loops on hook; repeat from ★ 5 times **more**, sc in next 12 chs, 3 sc in last ch; sc evenly across end of rows; working in sts across Row 150, 3 sc in first sc, sc in next 15 sts, 3 sc in next sc, (sc in next 14 sts, pull up a loop in next 3 sts, YO and draw through all 4 loops on hook, sc in next 14 sts, 3 sc in next sc) 6 times, sc in next 15 sts, 3 sc in last sc; join with slip st to first sc, finish off.

Hospitality

Visitors to your home will appreciate the warm welcome offered by this inviting wrap. Worked in strips, the design features pineapples, a traditional sign of hospitality.

Finished Size: 49¹/₂" x 64"

MATERIALS

Worsted Weight Yarn:
  Green - 17 ounces, (480 grams, 1,115 yards)
  Blue - 16 ounces, (450 grams, 1,050 yards)
  Aran - 15 ounces, (430 grams, 985 yards)
Crochet hook, size H (5.00 mm) **or** size needed for gauge

GAUGE: Each Strip = 4¹/₂"w

Gauge Swatch: 2"w x 3³/₄"h
Work same as First Pineapple.

STITCH GUIDE

SC DECREASE
Pull up a loop in each of next 2 sc, YO and draw through all 3 loops on hook **(counts as one sc)**.
TR DECREASE
YO twice, working in **front** of Rnd 3, insert hook in **front** 2 legs of sc *(Fig. 1)* on Rnd 2 **before** ch-4 sp, YO and pull up a loop, (YO and draw through 2 loops on hook) twice (2 loops on hook), YO twice, insert hook in **front** 2 legs of next sc **after** ch-4 sp, YO and pull up a loop, (YO and draw through 2 loops on hook) twice, YO and draw through all 3 loops on hook.

Fig. 1

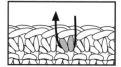

PICOT
Ch 2, slip st in top of sc just made *(Fig. 1, page 56)*.

Continued on page 92.

STRIP (Make 11)

FIRST PINEAPPLE

With Green, ch 10; join with slip st to form a ring.

Foundation Rnd (Right side): Ch 3, (6 dc, hdc, 10 sc, hdc) in ring; join with slip st to top of beginning ch-3: 19 sts.

Note: Loop a short piece of yarn around any stitch to mark Foundation Rnd as **right** side.

Begin working in rows.

Row 1: Ch 3 **(counts as first sp, now and throughout)**, place marker around ch-3 just made for st placement, sc in next dc, (ch 2, sc in next dc) 4 times, hdc in next dc **(counts as last sp, now and throughout)**, leave remaining 12 sts unworked: 6 sps.

Rows 2 and 3: Ch 3, **turn**; sc in next ch-2 sp, (ch 2, sc in next ch-2 sp) across to last sp, hdc in last sp: 4 sps.

Row 4: Ch 3, turn; sc in next ch-2 sp, ch 2, sc in next ch-2 sp, hdc in last sp: 3 sps.

Row 5: Ch 3, turn; sc in next ch-2 sp, hdc in last sp: 2 sps.

Row 6: Ch 3, turn; slip st in last sp, finish off: one ch-3 sp.

SECOND PINEAPPLE

Work same as First Pineapple through Row 5: 2 sps.

Row 6 (Joining row): Ch 1, turn; holding Pineapples with **right** sides together, slip st in ch-3 sp at point of **previous Pineapple**, ch 1, slip st in last sp on **new Pineapple**, finish off.

THIRD PINEAPPLE

With Green, ch 10; insert end of beginning ch-10 from **front** to **back** through ring of previous Pineapple, being careful not to twist ch, join with slip st to form a ring.

Work same as First Pineapple: one ch-3 sp.

REMAINING 15 PINEAPPLES

Repeat Second and Third Pineapples 7 times, then repeat Second Pineapple once **more**.

BORDER

Rnd 1: With **right** side of Pineapples facing and working in sps at end of rows, join Blue with slip st in marked row on First Pineapple; ch 1, 2 sc in same sp and in each of next 3 rows, † sc in next row, skip joining sps, sc in next row, 2 sc in each of next 4 rows, ch 4, skip next 3 sts on same Pineapple, [working through **both** thicknesses, sc in corresponding sc on both Pineapples, ch 4, skip next 3 sts on present Pineapple, working in sps at end of rows, 2 sc in each of next 4 rows, sc in next row, skip joining sps, sc in next row, 2 sc in each of next 4 rows, ch 4, skip next 3 sts on same Pineapple] 8 times, sc in next sc, ch 4, skip next sc, sc decrease, ch 4, skip next sc, sc in next sc, ch 4, skip next 3 sts †, 2 sc in each of next 4 rows, repeat from † to † once; join with slip st to first sc: 346 sc and 40 ch-4 sps.

Rnd 2: Ch 1, sc in same st and in next 4 sc, † ch 3, skip next 2 sc, sc in next sc, ch 4, skip next 2 sc, sc in next sc, ch 3, skip next 2 sc, sc in next 5 sc, ★ ch 3, sc in next ch-4 sp, ch 4, sc in next ch-4 sp, ch 3, sc in next 5 sc, ch 3, skip next 2 sc, sc in next sc, ch 4, skip next 2 sc, sc in next sc, ch 3, skip next 2 sc, sc in next 5 sc; repeat from ★ 7 times **more**, 5 sc in next ch-4 sp, (dc, ch 1) 4 times in next ch-4 sp, dc in next ch-4 sp, (ch 1, dc in same sp) 3 times, 5 sc in next ch-4 sp †, sc in next 5 sc, repeat from † to † once; join with slip st to first sc: 284 sts and 116 sps.

Rnd 3: Ch 1, sc in same st and in next 4 sc, † 2 sc in next ch-3 sp, 3 sc in next ch-4 sp, 2 sc in next ch-3 sp, ★ sc in next 5 sc, 2 sc in next ch-3 sp, 3 sc in next ch-4 sp, 2 sc in next ch-3 sp; repeat from ★ 15 times **more**, sc in next 10 sc, ch 2, (sc in next ch-1 sp, ch 2) 7 times, skip next dc †, sc in next 10 sc, repeat from † to † once, sc in last 5 sc; join with slip st to first sc, finish off: 452 sc and 16 ch-2 sps.

Rnd 4: With **right** side facing, join Aran with slip st in ch-2 sp **before** joining; ch 1, sc in same sp and in next 13 sc, † tr decrease, skip next sc on Rnd 3 from last sc made, ★ sc in next 11 sc, tr decrease, skip next sc on Rnd 3 from last sc made; repeat from ★ 15 times **more**, sc in next 13 sc and in next ch-2 sp, ch 2, sc in next ch-2 sp, dc in next ch-2 sp, (ch 1, dc in same sp) 3 times, sc in next ch-2 sp, ch 3, sc in next ch-2 sp, dc in next ch-2 sp, (ch 1, dc in same sp) 3 times, sc in next ch-2 sp, ch 2 †, sc in next ch-2 sp and in next 13 sc, repeat from † to † once; join with slip st to first sc: 466 sts and 18 sps.

Rnd 5: Ch 1, sc in same st and in each st across to next ch-2 sp, † 2 sc in ch-2 sp, sc in next sc and in next dc, (sc in next ch-1 sp, work Picot, sc in next dc) 3 times, (dc, ch 4, slip st in third ch from hook, ch 1, dc) in next ch-3 sp, skip next sc, sc in next dc, (sc in next ch-1 sp, work Picot, sc in next dc) 3 times, sc in next sc, 2 sc in next ch-2 sp †, sc in each st across to next ch-2 sp, repeat from † to † once; join with slip st to first sc, finish off.

ASSEMBLY

Holding long edge of 2 Strips with **wrong** sides together and working through **inside** loops only, join Aran with slip st in sixth sc **after** Picot; slip st in each sc across to within 5 sc of next Picot; finish off. Repeat for remaining Strips.

Fall Festival

With cooler temperatures and the turning of the leaves come fall festivals. This colorful cover-up reminds us to celebrate the simple pleasures of the season, such as the annual apple harvest.

Finished Size: 47$^{1}/_{2}$"x 64"

MATERIALS
Worsted Weight Yarn:
Black - 26$^{1}/_{2}$ ounces, (750 grams, 1,815 yards)
Purple - 8 ounces, (230 grams, 550 yards)
Blue - 8 ounces, (230 grams, 550 yards)
Pink - 8 ounces, (230 grams, 550 yards)
Green - 6 ounces, (170 grams, 410 yards)
Yellow - 5 ounces, (140 grams, 345 yards)
Crochet hook, size I (5.50 mm) **or** size needed for gauge

GAUGE: In pattern, 13 sts and 14 rows = 4"

Gauge Swatch: 4" square
Ch 14 **loosely**.
Row 1: Sc in second ch from hook and in each ch across: 13 sc.
Rows 2-14: Ch 1, turn; sc in each sc across.
Finish off.

Note: Each row is worked across length of Afghan. When joining yarn and finishing off, leave an 8" length to be worked into fringe.

AFGHAN BODY
With Green, ch 208 **loosely**.
Row 1 (Right side): Sc in second ch from hook and in each ch across; finish off: 207 sc.
Note: Loop a short piece of yarn around any stitch to mark Row 1 as **right** side.
Row 2: With **wrong** side facing, join Black with sc in first sc *(see Joining With Sc, page 140)*; ch 1, skip next sc, ★ (sc in next sc, ch 1, skip next sc) 3 times, sc in next 5 sc, ch 1, skip next sc; repeat from ★ across to last sc, sc in last sc; finish off: 138 sc and 69 ch-1 sps.
Row 3: With **right** side facing, join Green with sc in first sc; working in **front** of next ch-1 *(Fig. 18, page 141)*, dc in st one row **below**, ★ ch 1, skip next st, (sc in next sc, ch 1, skip next st) twice, working in **front** of next ch-1, dc in sc one row **below**, (sc in next sc, working in **front** of next ch-1, dc in st one row **below**) 3 times; repeat from ★ across to last sc, sc in last sc; finish off: 156 sts and 51 ch-1 sps.

Row 4: With **wrong** side facing, join Black with sc in first sc; ch 1, skip next dc, ★ (sc in next sc, ch 1, skip next dc) twice, sc in next 2 sts, working **behind** next ch-1, dc in st one row **below**, (sc in next sc, working **behind** next ch-1, dc in st one row **below**) twice, ch 1, skip next dc; repeat from ★ across to last sc, sc in last sc; finish off: 155 sts and 52 ch-1 sps.
Row 5: With **right** side facing, join Blue with sc in first sc; working in **front** of next ch-1, dc in dc one row **below**, ★ sc in next 2 sts, ch 1, skip next dc, (sc in next sc, ch 1, skip next st) twice, working in **front** of next ch-1, dc in dc one row **below**, (sc in next sc, working in **front** of next ch-1, dc in dc one row **below**) twice; repeat from ★ across to last sc, sc in last sc; finish off: 156 sts and 51 ch-1 sps.
Row 6: With **wrong** side facing, join Black with sc in first sc; ch 1, skip next dc, sc in next sc, ch 1, skip next dc, sc in next 2 sts, working **behind** next ch-1, dc in sc one row **below**, (sc in next sc, working **behind** next ch-1, dc in dc one row **below**) twice, ★ ch 1, skip next sc, (sc in next sc, ch 1, skip next dc) twice, sc in next 2 sts, working **behind** next ch-1, dc in sc one row **below**, (sc in next sc, working **behind** next ch-1, dc in dc one row **below**) twice; repeat from ★ across to last 4 sts, (ch 1, skip next st, sc in next sc) twice; finish off: 155 sts and 52 ch-1 sps.
Row 7: With **right** side facing, join Purple with sc in first sc; working in **front** of next ch-1, dc in dc one row **below**, sc in next sc, working in **front** of next ch-1, dc in sc one row **below**, sc in next 2 sts, ch 1, skip next dc, (sc in next sc, ch 1, skip next st) twice, ★ working in **front** of next ch-1, dc in dc one row **below**, (sc in next sc, working in **front** of next ch-1, dc in st one row **below**) twice, sc in next 2 sts, ch 1, skip next dc, (sc in next sc, ch 1, skip next st) twice; repeat from ★ across to last 2 ch-1 sps, (working in **front** of next ch-1, dc in dc one row **below**, sc in next sc) twice; finish off: 156 sts and 51 ch-1 sps.
Row 8: With **wrong** side facing, join Black with sc in first sc; ch 1, skip next dc, ★ sc in next 2 sts, working **behind** next ch-1, dc in sc one row **below**, (sc in next sc, working **behind** next ch-1, dc in dc one row **below**) twice, ch 1, skip next sc, (sc in next sc, ch 1, skip next dc) twice; repeat from ★ across to last sc, sc in last sc; finish off: 155 sts and 52 ch-1 sps.

Continued on page 94.

Row 9: With **right** side facing, join Pink with sc in first sc; working in **front** of next ch-1, dc in dc one row **below**, ★ (sc in next sc, working in **front** of next ch-1, dc in st one row **below**) twice, sc in next 2 sts, ch 1, skip next dc, (sc in next sc, ch 1, skip next st) twice, working in **front** of next ch-1, dc in dc one row **below**; repeat from ★ across to last sc, sc in last sc; finish off: 156 sts and 51 ch-1 sps.

Row 10: With **wrong** side facing, join Black with sc in first sc; ch 1, skip next dc, ★ working **behind** next ch-1, dc in sc one row **below**, (sc in next sc, working **behind** next ch-1, dc in dc one row **below**) twice, ch 1, skip next sc, (sc in next sc, ch 1, skip next dc) 3 times; repeat from ★ across to last sc, sc in last sc; finish off: 138 sts and 69 ch-1 sps.

Row 11: With **right** side facing, join Yellow with sc in first sc; working in **front** of next ch-1, dc in dc one row **below**, ★ (sc in next sc, working in **front** of next ch-1, dc in st one row **below**) 3 times, ch 1, skip next dc, (sc in next sc, ch 1, skip next dc) twice, working in **front** of next ch-1, dc in dc one row **below**; repeat from ★ across to last sc, sc in last sc; finish off: 156 sts and 51 ch-1 sps.

Row 12: With **wrong** side facing, join Black with sc in first sc; ch 1, skip next dc, ★ working **behind** next ch-1, dc in dc one row **below**, (sc in next sc, working **behind** next ch-1, dc in dc one row **below**) twice, sc in next 2 sts, ch 1, skip next dc, (sc in next sc, ch 1, skip next dc) twice; repeat from ★ across to last sc, sc in last sc; finish off: 155 sts and 52 ch-1 sps.

Row 13: With **right** side facing, join Pink with sc in first sc; working in **front** of next ch-1, dc in dc one row **below**, ★ (sc in next sc, working in **front** of next ch-1, dc in dc one row **below**) twice, ch 1, skip next sc, (sc in next sc, ch 1, skip next dc) twice, sc in next 2 sts, working in **front** of next ch-1, dc in dc one row **below**; repeat from ★ across to last sc, sc in last sc; finish off: 156 sts and 51 ch-1 sps.

Row 14: With **wrong** side facing, join Black with sc in first sc; ch 1, skip next dc, sc in next sc, ch 1, skip next sc, working **behind** next ch-1, dc in dc one row **below**, (sc in next sc, working **behind** next ch-1, dc in st one row **below**) twice, sc in next 2 sts, ★ ch 1, skip next dc, (sc in next sc, ch 1, skip next st) twice, working **behind** next ch-1, dc in dc one row **below**, (sc in next sc, working **behind** next ch-1, dc in st one row **below**) twice, sc in next 2 sts; repeat from ★ across to last 4 sts, (ch 1, skip next dc, sc in next sc) twice; finish off: 155 sts and 52 ch-1 sps.

Row 15: With **right** side facing, join Purple with sc in first sc; working in **front** of next ch-1, dc in dc one row **below**, sc in next sc, working in **front** of next ch-1, dc in dc one row **below**, ch 1, skip next sc, (sc in next sc, ch 1, skip next dc) twice, sc in next

2 sts, ★ working in **front** of next ch-1, dc in sc one row **below**, (sc in next sc, working in **front** of next ch-1, dc in dc one row **below**) twice, ch 1, skip next sc, (sc in next sc, ch 1, skip next dc) twice, sc in next 2 sts; repeat from ★ across to last 2 ch-1 sps, (working in **front** of next ch-1, dc in st one row **below**, sc in next sc) twice; finish off: 156 sts and 51 ch-1 sps.

Row 16: With **wrong** side facing, join Black with sc in first sc; ★ ch 1, skip next dc, (sc in next sc, ch 1, skip next st) twice, working **behind** next ch-1, dc in dc one row **below**, (sc in next sc, working **behind** next ch-1, dc in st one row **below**) twice, sc in next 2 sts; repeat from ★ across to last 2 sts, ch 1, skip next dc, sc in last sc; finish off: 155 sts and 52 ch-1 sps.

Row 17: With **right** side facing, join Blue with sc in first sc; working in **front** of next ch-1, dc in dc one row **below**, ★ ch 1, skip next sc, (sc in next sc, ch 1, skip next dc) twice, sc in next 2 sts, working in **front** of next ch-1, dc in sc one row **below**, (sc in next sc, working in **front** of next ch-1, dc in dc one row **below**) twice; repeat from ★ across to last sc, sc in last sc; finish off: 156 sts and 51 ch-1 sps.

Row 18: With **wrong** side facing, join Black with sc in first sc; ch 1, skip next dc, ★ (sc in next sc, ch 1, skip next st) 3 times, working **behind** next ch-1, dc in dc one row **below**, (sc in next sc, working **behind** next ch-1, dc in st one row **below**) twice, ch 1, skip next dc; repeat from ★ across to last sc, sc in last sc; finish off: 138 sts and 69 ch-1 sps.

Rows 19-162: Repeat Rows 3-18, 9 times.

Row 163: With **right** side facing, join Green with sc in first sc; working in **front** of next ch-1, dc in dc one row **below**, ★ sc in next 5 sts, working in **front** of next ch-1, dc in sc one row **below**, (sc in next sc, working in **front** of next ch-1, dc in dc one row **below**) 3 times; repeat from ★ across to last sc, sc in last sc; finish off: 207 sts.

TRIM
FIRST SIDE

Row 1: With **wrong** side facing, join Black with sc in first sc on Row 163; sc in next dc, ch 1, ★ skip next st, sc in next st, ch 1; repeat from ★ across to last 3 sts, skip next sc, sc in last 2 sts; do **not** finish off: 105 sc and 102 ch-1 sps.

Row 2: Ch 1, turn; slip st in first sc, ch 1, skip next sc, (slip st in next ch-1 sp, ch 1) across to last 2 sc, skip next sc, slip st in last sc; finish off.

Continued on page 96.

SECOND SIDE

Row 1: With **wrong** side facing and working in free loops of beginning ch *(Fig. 17b, page 141)*, join Black with sc in ch at base of first sc; sc in next ch, ch 1, ★ skip next ch, sc in next ch, ch 1; repeat from ★ across to last 3 chs, skip next ch, sc in last 2 chs; do **not** finish off: 105 sc and 102 ch-1 sps.

Row 2: Ch 1, turn; slip st in first sc, ch 1, skip next sc, (slip st in next ch-1 sp, ch 1) across to last 2 sc, skip next sc, slip st in last sc; finish off.

Holding 3 strands of Black and 3 strands of corresponding color yarn together, each 17" long, add additional fringe in every other row across short edges of Afghan *(Figs. 22b & d, page 142)*.

Remnants

There's no reason why you can't do a little spring cleaning this fall and use the remnants from your yarn closet to make an intriguing afghan. Kids especially enjoy vivid creations like this one.

Finished Size: 42" x 58"

MATERIALS

Worsted Weight Yarn:
    Black - 12^1/$_2$ ounces, (360 grams, 705 yards)
    Scraps - 30 ounces,
        (850 grams, 1,695 yards) **total**
        Note: Each Scrap row requires 34 yards.
    Crochet hook, size I (5.50 mm) **or** size needed for gauge

GAUGE: In pattern, 5 Clusters = 4";
            7 rows = 3^7/$_8$"

Gauge Swatch: 4^1/$_2$"w x 3^7/$_8$"h
Ch 19 **loosely**.
Work same as Afghan for 7 rows.

STITCH GUIDE

CLUSTER (uses next 3 dc)
★ YO, insert hook in **next** dc, YO and pull up a loop, YO and draw through 2 loops on hook; repeat from ★ 2 times **more**, YO and draw through all 4 loops on hook *(Figs. 12a & b, page 139)*.

Note: Each row is worked across length of Afghan. When joining yarn and finishing off, leave an 8" end to be worked into fringe.

To work **color change**, work the last st to within one step of completion, cut yarn, hook new yarn and draw through all loops on hook *(Fig. 19, page 141)*.

AFGHAN

With Black, ch 217 **loosely**.

Row 1 (Right side): (Dc, ch 1, dc) in fifth ch from hook, ★ skip next 2 chs, (dc, ch 1, dc) in next ch; repeat from ★ across to last 2 chs, skip next ch, dc in last ch changing to Scrap color desired: 144 sts and 71 ch-1 sps.

Note: Loop a short piece of yarn around any stitch to mark Row 1 as **right** side.

Row 2: Ch 3 **(counts as first dc, now and throughout)**, turn; 3 dc in each ch-1 sp across to last dc, skip last dc, dc in next ch: 215 dc.

Row 3: Ch 4 **(counts as first dc plus ch 1, now and throughout)**, turn; work Cluster, (ch 2, work Cluster) across to last dc, ch 1, dc in last dc changing to Black: 71 Clusters and 72 sps.

Row 4: Ch 3, turn; (dc, ch 1, dc) in each Cluster across to last dc, dc in last dc changing to Scrap color desired: 144 dc and 71 ch-1 sps.

Row 5: Ch 3, turn; 3 dc in each ch-1 sp across to last 2 dc, skip next dc, dc in last dc: 215 dc.

Row 6: Ch 4, turn; work Cluster, (ch 2, work Cluster) across to last dc, ch 1, dc in last dc changing to Black: 71 Clusters and 72 sps.

Rows 7-75: Repeat Rows 4-6, 23 times.

Row 76: Ch 3, turn; (dc, ch 1, dc) in each Cluster across to last dc, dc in last dc; finish off.

Add additional fringe across short edges of Afghan *(Figs. 22b & d, page 142)* for a total of 10 strands of corresponding color and 11 strands of Black, each 17" long.

Mums Galore

Fall's most popular flower — the mum — is in full bloom on this beautiful throw. The pattern is worked in squares, and a delicate green edging complements the delightful bouquet.

Finished Size: 50" x 64"

MATERIALS
Worsted Weight Yarn:
Tan - 29^1/$_2$ ounces, (840 grams, 1,935 yards)
Rust - 13 ounces, (370 grams, 855 yards)
Green - 12 ounces, (340 grams, 785 yards)
Crochet hook, size H (5.00 mm) **or** size needed for gauge
Yarn needle

GAUGE: Each Square = 7"

Gauge Swatch: 4^1/$_2$" square
Work same as Square through Rnd 4.

STITCH GUIDE

2-DC CLUSTER
Ch 3, 2 dc in third ch from hook.
BEGINNING 3-DC CLUSTER
(uses one st or sp)
Ch 2, ★ YO, insert hook in st or sp indicated, YO and pull up a loop, YO and draw through 2 loops on hook; repeat from ★ once **more**, YO and draw through all 3 loops on hook (*Figs. 11a & b, page 139*).
3-DC CLUSTER (uses one st or sp)
★ YO, insert hook in st or sp indicated, YO and pull up a loop, YO and draw through 2 loops on hook; repeat from ★ 2 times **more**, YO and draw through all 4 loops on hook (*Figs. 11a & b, page 139*).

SQUARE (Make 63)

With Rust, ch 4; join with slip st to form a ring.
Rnd 1 (Right side): Ch 4, (dc in ring, ch 1) 7 times; join with slip st to third ch of beginning ch-4, finish off: 8 sts and 8 ch-1 sps.
Note: Loop a short piece of yarn around any stitch to mark Rnd 1 as **right** side.
Rnd 2: With **right** side facing, join Green with sc in any ch-1 sp (*see Joining With Sc, page 140*); ch 3, (sc in next ch-1 sp, ch 3) around; join with slip st to first sc, finish off.

Rnd 3: With **right** side facing, join Tan with slip st in any ch-3 sp; work Beginning 3-dc Cluster in same sp, work 2-dc Cluster, dc in next ch-3 sp, work 2-dc Cluster, ★ work 3-dc Cluster in next ch-3 sp, work 2-dc Cluster, dc in next ch-3 sp, work 2-dc Cluster; repeat from ★ 2 times **more**; join with slip st to top of Beginning 3-dc Cluster, do **not** finish off: 4 dc and 12 Clusters.
Rnd 4: Work Beginning 3-dc Cluster in same st, ch 3, skip next 2-dc Cluster, tr in next dc, (ch 2, tr in same st) twice, ch 3, skip next 2-dc Cluster, ★ work 3-dc Cluster in next 3-dc Cluster, ch 3, skip next 2-dc Cluster, tr in next dc, (ch 2, tr in same st) twice, ch 3, skip next 2-dc Cluster; repeat from ★ 2 times **more**; join with slip st to top of Beginning 3-dc Cluster, finish off: 12 tr, 4 Clusters, and 16 sps.
Rnd 5: With **right** side facing, join Green with sc in center tr of any corner 3-tr group; (ch 1, sc in same st) twice, 2 sc in next ch-2 sp, sc in next tr, 3 sc in next ch-3 sp, sc in next Cluster, 3 sc in next ch-3 sp, sc in next tr, 2 sc in next ch-2 sp, ★ sc in next tr, (ch 1, sc in same st) twice, 2 sc in next ch-2 sp, sc in next tr, 3 sc in next ch-3 sp, sc in next Cluster, 3 sc in next ch-3 sp, sc in next tr, 2 sc in next ch-2 sp; repeat from ★ 2 times **more**; join with slip st to first sc, finish off: 64 sc and 8 ch-1 sps.
Rnd 6: With **right** side facing, join Rust with slip st in center sc of any corner 3-sc group; ch 3 (**counts as first dc**), (2 dc, ch 3, 3 dc) in same st, skip next ch-1 sp, dc in next 15 sc, skip next ch-1 sp, ★ (3 dc, ch 3, 3 dc) in next sc, skip next ch-1 sp, dc in next 15 sc, skip next ch-1 sp; repeat from ★ 2 times **more**; join with slip st to first dc, finish off: 84 dc.
Rnd 7: With **right** side facing, join Green with sc in any corner ch-3 sp; 2 sc in same sp, ch 1, skip next dc, (sc in next dc, ch 1, skip next dc) across to next corner ch-3 sp, ★ 3 sc in corner ch-3 sp, ch 1, skip next dc, (sc in next dc, ch 1, skip next dc) across to next corner ch-3 sp; repeat from ★ 2 times **more**; join with slip st to first sc, finish off: 52 sc and 44 ch-1 sps.
Rnd 8: With **right** side facing, join Tan with slip st in center sc of any corner 3-sc group; work (Beginning 3-dc Cluster, ch 3, 3-dc Cluster) in same st, ch 1, (work 3-dc Cluster in next ch-1 sp, ch 1) across to

next corner 3-sc group, skip next sc, ★ work (3-dc Cluster, ch 3, 3-dc Cluster) in next sc, ch 1, (work 3-dc Cluster in next ch-1 sp, ch 1) across to next corner 3-sc group, skip next sc; repeat from ★ 2 times **more**; join with slip st to top of Beginning 3-dc Cluster, finish off: 52 3-dc Clusters and 52 sps.

ASSEMBLY

With Tan and working through **both** loops, whipstitch Squares together *(Fig. 21b, page 142)*, forming 7 vertical strips of 9 Squares each, beginning in center ch of first corner ch-3 and ending in center ch of next corner ch-3; whipstitch strips together in same manner.

EDGING

With **right** side facing, join Green with sc in any corner ch-3 sp; ch 3, sc in same sp, ch 3, (sc in next sp, ch 3) across to next corner ch-3 sp, ★ (sc, ch 3) twice in corner sp, (sc in next sp, ch 3) across to next corner ch-3 sp; repeat from ★ 2 times **more**; join with slip st to first sc, finish off.

Fall Breeze

As pretty as the changing leaves rustling in a fall breeze, this afghan has captivating appeal. The quick-to-stitch design is crocheted using a Q hook and holding two strands of yarn together.

Finished Size: 49" x 63"

MATERIALS
Worsted Weight Yarn:
    Variegated - 26 ounces, (740 grams, 1,580 yards)
    Brown - 26 ounces, (740 grams, 1,580 yards)
Crochet hook, size Q (15.00 mm)

Note: Afghan is worked holding two strands of yarn together.

GAUGE: In pattern,
      one repeat (point to point) = $9^1/2$";
      6 rows = $4^1/2$"

Gauge Swatch: $4^1/2$"w x $3^1/2$"h
Ch 9 **loosely**.
Row 1: Sc in second ch from hook and in each ch across: 8 sc.
Rows 2-6: Ch 1, turn; sc in Back Loop Only of each sc across *(Fig. 16, page 141)*.
Finish off.

AFGHAN BODY
With Variegated, ch 120 **loosely**.
Row 1 (Right side): Sc in second ch from hook and in next ch, skip next ch, sc in next 10 chs, 3 sc in next ch, sc in next 10 chs, ★ skip next 2 chs, sc in next 10 chs, 3 sc in next ch, sc in next 10 chs; repeat from ★ across to last 3 chs, skip next ch, sc in last 2 chs: 119 sc.
Note: Loop a short piece of yarn around any stitch to mark Row 1 as **right** side.
Rows 2-9: Ch 1, turn; sc in first 2 sc, skip next sc, working in Back Loops Only *(Fig. 16, page 141)*, sc in next 10 sc, 3 sc in next sc, sc in next 10 sc, ★ skip next 2 sc, sc in next 10 sc, 3 sc in next sc, sc in next 10 sc; repeat from ★ across to last 3 sc, skip next sc, sc in **both** loops of last 2 sc.
Finish off.

Row 10: With **right** side facing, join Brown with sc in both loops of first sc *(see Joining With Sc, page 140)*; sc in next sc, skip next sc, working in Back Loops Only, sc in next 10 sc, 3 sc in next sc, sc in next 10 sc, ★ skip next 2 sc, sc in next 10 sc, 3 sc in next sc, sc in next 10 sc; repeat from ★ across to last 3 sc, skip next sc, sc in **both** loops of last 2 sc.
Rows 11-18: Ch 1, turn; sc in first 2 sc, skip next sc, working in Back Loops Only, sc in next 10 sc, 3 sc in next sc, sc in next 10 sc, ★ skip next 2 sc, sc in next 10 sc, 3 sc in next sc, sc in next 10 sc; repeat from ★ across to last 3 sc, skip next sc, sc in **both** loops of last 2 sc; at end of Row 18, finish off.
Rows 19-27: With Variegated, repeat Rows 10-18.
Rows 28-81: Repeat Rows 10-27, 3 times.

EDGING
Rnd 1: With **right** side facing and working in both loops, join Brown with slip st in first sc on Row 81; ch 2, 2 hdc in same st, hdc in next sc, skip next sc, hdc in next 10 sc, 3 hdc in next sc, hdc in next 10 sc, ★ skip next 2 sc, hdc in next 10 sc, 3 hdc in next sc, hdc in next 10 sc; repeat from ★ across to last 3 sc, skip next sc, hdc in next sc, 3 hdc in last sc; working in end of rows, skip first row, hdc in next row and in each row across; working in sps and in free loops of beginning ch *(Fig. 17b, page 141)*, 3 hdc in first ch, hdc in next 12 chs, skip next ch, (hdc in next 10 chs, 3 hdc in next ch-2 sp, hdc in next 10 chs, skip next ch) 4 times, hdc in next 12 chs, 3 hdc in next ch; hdc in end of each row across to last row, skip last row; join with slip st to top of beginning ch-2.
Rnd 2: Ch 1, working from **left** to **right**, work reverse sc in each st around *(Figs. 15a-d, page 140)*; join with slip st to first st, finish off.

WINTER

With winter comes a host of seasonal pleasantries. It's a time for enjoying the frosty charm of a horse-drawn sleigh ride through the snow, curling up with a loved one in front of a crackling fire, and celebrating the holidays with friends and family. Our winter wraps are ideal for keeping you warm whether you're indoors or out, and they also make excellent Christmas gifts.

Memories

Great for making with yarn scraps, this afghan is a memory maker. Snuggling up in it will bring to mind the sweaters and other projects that were made from each color.

Finished Size: 49" x 68"

MATERIALS
Worsted Weight Yarn:
    Black - 42 ounces, (1,190 grams, 2,375 yards)
    Scraps - 34 ounces, (970 grams, 1,920 yards) **total**
      Note: We used 8 different colors.
Crochet hook, size I (5.50 mm) **or** size needed for
    gauge
Yarn needle

GAUGE: Each Strip = $1^1/2$" wide
            In pattern, (sc, ch 1) 7 times = 4"

Gauge Swatch: $4^1/4$"w x $1^1/2$"h
With Scrap color, ch 16.
Work same as Strip.

Note: When joining yarn and finishing off, leave an 11" length to be worked into fringe.

STRIP (Make 32)
FIRST SIDE
With Scrap color, ch 240.
Row 1 (Right side): Sc in second ch from hook, ★ ch 1, skip next ch, sc in next ch; repeat from ★ across: 120 sc and 119 ch-1 sps.
Note: Loop a short piece of yarn around last sc made to mark Row 1 as **right** side and bottom edge.
Row 2: Ch 1, turn; sc in first sc, (ch 1, sc in next sc) across; finish off.
Row 3: With **right** side facing, join Black with sc in first sc *(see Joining With Sc, page 140)*; working in **front** of next ch-1 *(Fig. 18, page 141)*, dc in ch-1 sp one row **below**, sc in next sc, ★ working **behind** next ch-1, dc in ch-1 sp one row **below**, sc in next sc, working in **front** of next ch-1, dc in ch-1 sp one row **below**, sc in next sc; repeat from ★ across; finish off: 239 sts.

SECOND SIDE
Row 1: With **wrong** side facing and working in free loops of beginning ch *(Fig. 17b, page 141)*, join **same** Scrap color as First Side with sc in ch at base of first sc; ★ ch 1, skip next ch, sc in next ch; repeat from ★ across; finish off.
Row 2: Work same as First Side Row 3.

ASSEMBLY
With Black, holding bottom edges at same end and working through both loops, whipstitch Strips together *(Fig. 21b, page 142)*, beginning in first sc and ending in last sc.

TRIM
FIRST SIDE
Row 1: With **wrong** side facing and working across long edge, join Black with sc in first sc; sc in next dc, ch 1, ★ skip next sc, sc in next dc, ch 1; repeat from ★ across to last 3 sts, skip next sc, sc in last 2 sts.
Row 2: Ch 1, turn; slip st in first sc, ch 1, (slip st in next ch-1 sp, ch 1) across to last 2 sc, skip next sc, slip st in last sc; finish off.

SECOND SIDE
Work same as First Side.

Holding 7 strands of Black **and** 3 strands of corresponding color yarn together, each 23" long, add additional fringe in each color stripe across short edges of Afghan *(Figs. 22b & d, page 142)*.

Snow on the Pines

This majestic wrap resembles the breathtaking beauty of a mountain of snow-capped pine trees. Long double crochet stitches enhance the likeness.

Finished Size: 45¹/₂" x 60"

MATERIALS

Worsted Weight Yarn:
   Dk Green - 29 ounces, (820 grams, 1,640 yards)
   Ecru - 20 ounces, (570 grams, 1,130 yards)
   Green - 20 ounces, (570 grams, 1,130 yards)
Crochet hook, size I (5.50 mm) **or** size needed for gauge

GAUGE: In pattern, 13 sts = 4"; Rows 7-18 = 3¹/₂"

Gauge Swatch: 8³/₄"w x 4"h
Ch 32 **loosely**.
Work same as Afghan for 12 rows.

STITCH GUIDE

> **LONG DOUBLE CROCHET**
> *(abbreviated LDC)*
> Working **around** previous row(s), YO, insert hook in ch-1 sp indicated, YO and pull up a loop even with last st made (3 loops on hook), (YO and draw through 2 loops on hook) twice *(Fig. 9, page 139)*.

AFGHAN

With Dk Green, ch 152 **loosely**, place marker in second ch from hook for st placement.
Row 1 (Right side): Dc in sixth ch from hook, ★ ch 1, skip next ch, dc in next ch; repeat from ★ across: 74 dc and 74 sps.
Note: Loop a short piece of yarn around any stitch to mark Row 1 as **right** side.
Row 2: Ch 1, turn; sc in first dc and in next ch-1 sp, (sc in next dc and in next ch-1 sp) 3 times, ch 1, ★ sc in next ch-1 sp, (sc in next dc and in next ch-1 sp) 5 times, ch 1; repeat from ★ across to last 4 sps, (sc in next ch-1 sp and in next dc) 3 times, sc in next sp and in marked ch: 137 sc and 12 ch-1 sps.
Row 3: Ch 1, turn; sc in first 7 sc, ch 1, sc in next ch-1 sp, ch 1, ★ skip next sc, sc in next 9 sc, ch 1, sc in next ch-1 sp, ch 1; repeat from ★ across to last 8 sc, skip next sc, sc in last 7 sc: 125 sc and 24 ch-1 sps.
Row 4: Ch 1, turn; sc in first 6 sc, ch 1, sc in next ch-1 sp, sc in next sc and in next ch-1 sp, ch 1, ★ skip next sc, sc in next 7 sc, ch 1, sc in next ch-1 sp, sc in next sc and in next ch-1 sp, ch 1; repeat from ★ across to last 7 sc, skip next sc, sc in last 6 sc.
Row 5: Ch 1, turn; sc in first 5 sc, ★ ch 1, sc in next ch-1 sp, sc in next 3 sc and in next ch-1 sp, ch 1, skip next sc, sc in next 5 sc; repeat from ★ across.
Row 6: Ch 3 **(counts as first dc, now and throughout)**, turn; dc in next sc and in each sc and each ch-1 sp across; finish off: 149 dc.
Row 7: With **right** side facing, join Green with sc in first dc *(see Joining With Sc, page 140)*; sc in next 4 dc, ★ work LDC in ch-1 sp one row **below** next dc, work LDC in ch-1 sp 2 rows **below** next dc, work LDC in ch-1 sp 3 rows **below** next dc, work LDC in ch-1 sp 4 rows **below** next dc, work LDC in ch-1 sp 3 rows **below** next dc, work LDC in ch-1 sp 2 rows **below** next dc, work LDC in ch-1 sp one row **below** next dc, sc in next 5 dc; repeat from ★ across.
Row 8: Ch 1, turn; sc in first 8 sts, ch 1, ★ skip next LDC, sc in next 11 sts, ch 1; repeat from ★ across to last 9 sts, skip next LDC, sc in last 8 sts: 137 sc and 12 ch-1 sps.
Row 9: Ch 1, turn; sc in first 7 sc, ch 1, sc in next ch-1 sp, ch 1, ★ skip next sc, sc in next 9 sc, ch 1, sc in next ch-1 sp, ch 1; repeat from ★ across to last 8 sc, skip next sc, sc in last 7 sc: 125 sc and 24 ch-1 sps.
Row 10: Ch 1, turn; sc in first 6 sc, ch 1, sc in next ch-1 sp, sc in next sc and in next ch-1 sp, ch 1, ★ skip next sc, sc in next 7 sc, ch 1, sc in next ch-1 sp, sc in next sc and in next ch-1 sp, ch 1; repeat from ★ across to last 7 sc, skip next sc, sc in last 6 sc.
Row 11: Ch 1, turn; sc in first 5 sc, ★ ch 1, sc in next ch-1 sp, sc in next 3 sc and in next ch-1 sp, ch 1, skip next sc, sc in next 5 sc; repeat from ★ across.
Row 12: Ch 3, turn; dc in next sc and in each sc and each ch-1 sp across; finish off: 149 dc.
Rows 13-18: With Ecru, repeat Rows 7-12.
Rows 19-24: With Dk Green, repeat Rows 7-12.
Rows 25-203: Repeat Rows 7-24, 9 times; then repeat Rows 7-23 once **more**.
Row 204: Ch 4, turn; skip next sc, dc in next sc, ★ ch 1, skip next st, dc in next st; repeat from ★ across; finish off.

Holding 6 strands of Dk Green yarn together, each 15" long, add fringe in each sp across short edges of Afghan *(Figs. 22a & c, page 142)*.

Cozy Classic

When cold weather keeps you indoors, reach for this classic comforter. The pattern's intriguing combination of stitches makes it extra plush and warm.

Finished Size: 49" x 62^1/$_2$"

MATERIALS
Worsted Weight Yarn:
    Dk Grey - 29 ounces, (820 grams, 1,805 yards)
    Grey - 15^1/$_2$ ounces, (440 grams, 965 yards)
Crochet hook, size I (5.50 mm) **or** size needed
    for gauge
Yarn needle

GAUGE: Each Strip = 4" wide;
             6 rows = 4^1/$_2$"

Gauge Swatch: 2^3/$_4$"w x 4^1/$_2$"h
Work same as Center through Row 6.
Finish off.

STITCH GUIDE

CLUSTER (uses one st or sp)
★ YO, insert hook in st or sp indicated, YO and pull up a loop, YO and draw through 2 loops on hook; repeat from ★ once **more**, YO and draw through all 3 loops on hook (*Figs. 11a & b, page 139*).
LONG DOUBLE CROCHET
  (*abbreviated LDC*)
YO, insert hook around posts of sts indicated, YO and pull up a loop even with last st made (3 loops on hook), (YO and draw through 2 loops on hook) twice (*Fig. 9, page 139*).
CROSS STITCH (*abbreviated Cross St*)
Work LDC in next row, working **around** LDC just made, work LDC in same row as first leg of last Cross St made.

STRIP (Make 12)
CENTER
With Dk Grey, ch 12 **loosely**.
Row 1 (Right side): Dc in fourth ch from hook **(3 skipped chs count as first dc)**, skip next 2 chs, work 2 Clusters in next ch, ch 2, work 2 Clusters in next ch, skip next 2 chs, dc in last 2 chs: 8 sts and one ch-2 sp.

Note: Loop a short piece of yarn around any stitch to mark Row 1 as **right** side and bottom edge.
Row 2: Ch 3 **(counts as first dc, now and throughout)**, turn; dc in next dc, (2 dc, ch 2, 2 dc) in next ch-2 sp, skip next 2 Clusters, dc in last 2 dc.
Row 3: Ch 3, turn; dc in next dc, skip next dc, sc in sp **before** next dc (*Fig. 20, page 141*), work (2 Clusters, ch 2, 2 Clusters) in next ch-2 sp, skip next dc, sc in sp **before** next dc, skip next dc, dc in last 2 dc: 10 sts and one ch-2 sp.
Row 4: Ch 3, turn; dc in next dc, (2 dc, ch 2, 2 dc) in next ch-2 sp, skip next 3 sts, dc in last 2 dc: 8 dc and one ch-2 sp.
Rows 5-77: Repeat Rows 3 and 4, 36 times; then repeat Row 3 once **more**.
Row 78: Ch 3, turn; dc in next dc, ch 2, 2 sc in next ch-2 sp, ch 2, skip next 3 sts, dc in last 2 dc; finish off.

BORDER
With **right** side facing, join Grey with sc in first dc on Row 78 (*see Joining With Sc, page 140*); 2 sc in same st, sc in next dc, 2 sc in next ch-2 sp, sc in next 2 sc, 2 sc in next ch-2 sp, sc in next dc, 3 sc in last dc; † working **around** posts of first 2 dc at end of rows, skip first row, work LDC in next row, working **around** LDC just made, work LDC in skipped row **(first Cross St made)**, work Cross Sts across †; working in sps and in free loops of beginning ch (*Fig. 17b, page 141*), 3 sc in first ch, sc in next ch, 2 sc in next sp, sc in next 2 chs, 2 sc in next sp, sc in next ch, 3 sc in next ch; repeat from † to † once; join with slip st to first sc, finish off: 154 Cross Sts and 28 sc.

ASSEMBLY
With Grey and working through inside loops only, whipstitch long edge of Strips together (*Fig. 21a, page 142*), beginning in center sc of first corner 3-sc group and ending in center sc of next corner 3-sc group.

Continued on page 110.

EDGING

Rnd 1: With **right** side facing and working across long edge, join Grey with sc in center sc of first corner 3-sc group; ch 1, sc in same st and in next sc, † (skip next LDC, sc in next LDC, working **around** sc just made, sc in skipped LDC) across to next corner 3-sc group, sc in next sc, (sc, ch 1, sc) in center sc, ch 2, skip next sc, dc in next sc, ch 2, skip next 2 sc, (2 tr in next sc, ch 2) twice, skip next 2 sc, dc in next sc, ch 2, skip next sc, ★ sc in same sc as joining on same Strip, sc in joining and in same sc as joining on next Strip, ch 2, skip next sc, dc in next sc, ch 2, skip next 2 sc, (2 tr in next sc, ch 2) twice, skip next 2 sc, dc in next sc, ch 2, skip next sc; repeat from ★ across to center sc of next corner 3-sc group †, (sc, ch 1, sc) in center sc, sc in next sc, repeat from † to † once; join with slip st to first sc: 530 sts and 124 sps.

Rnd 2: Slip st in first corner ch-1 sp, ch 1, (sc, ch 1) twice in same sp, † skip next sc, (slip st in next sc, ch 1) across to within one sc of next corner ch-1 sp, skip next sc, (sc, ch 1) twice in corner ch-1 sp, (sc, ch 2, sc) in next 2 ch-2 sps, (sc, ch 3, sc, ch 5, sc, ch 3, sc) in next ch-2 sp, (sc, ch 2, sc) in next 2 ch-2 sps, ★ skip next sc, slip st in next sc, (sc, ch 2, sc) in next 2 ch-2 sps, (sc, ch 3, sc, ch 5, sc, ch 3, sc) in next ch-2 sp, (sc, ch 2, sc) in next 2 ch-2 sps; repeat from ★ across to next corner ch-1 sp, ch 1 †, (sc, ch 1) twice in corner ch-1 sp, repeat from † to † once; join with slip st to first sc, finish off.

Hearthside Stripes

Need a nice, heavy afghan for relaxing by the fireplace on a chilly winter day? This one is quick to crochet using a Q hook and holding two strands of yarn together.

Finished Size: 46" x 61"

MATERIALS
Worsted Weight Yarn:
    Green - 46 ounces, (1,310 grams, 2,005 yards)
    Ecru - 20 ounces, (570 grams, 870 yards)
    Rose - 10 ounces, (280 grams, 435 yards)
Crochet hook, size Q (15.00 mm)

GAUGE: 8 sc = $4^1/2$"; 8 rows = 4"

Gauge Swatch: $4^1/2$"w x $3^1/4$"h
Ch 9 **loosely.**
Work same as Afghan for 6 rows.
Finish off.

Note: Each row is worked across length of Afghan holding two strands of yarn together. When joining yarn and finishing off, leave a 9" end to be worked into fringe.

AFGHAN

With Green, ch 110 **loosely.**
Row 1 (Right side): Sc in back ridge of second ch from hook and each ch across *(Fig. 2b, page 137)*: 109 sc.

Note: Loop a short piece of yarn around any stitch to mark Row 1 as **right** side.
Rows 2-8: Ch 1, turn; sc in each sc across; at end of Row 8, finish off.
Row 9: With **right** side facing, join Ecru with sc in first sc *(see Joining With Sc, page 140)*; sc in next sc and in each sc across.
Row 10: Ch 1, turn; sc in each sc across; finish off.
Row 11: With **right** side facing, join Rose with sc in first sc; sc in next sc and in each sc across.
Row 12: Ch 1, turn; sc in each sc across; finish off.
Row 13: With **right** side facing, join Ecru with sc in first sc; sc in next sc and in each sc across.
Row 14: Ch 1, turn; sc in each sc across; finish off.
Row 15: With **right** side facing, join Green with sc in first sc; sc in next sc and in each sc across.
Rows 16-22: Ch 1, turn; sc in each sc across; at end of Row 22, finish off.
Repeat Rows 9-22 until Afghan measures approximately 46" from beginning ch, ending by working Row 22.

Holding 11 strands of corresponding color yarn together, each 19" long, add additional fringe evenly across short edges of Afghan *(Figs. 22b & d, page 142)*.

Angels All Around

Symbolizing the messenger who brought tidings of Jesus' birth, this divine afghan makes a wonderful holiday wrap. The angels on its squares will serve as a daily reminder of that joyous event.

Finished Size: 46" x 61"

MATERIALS
Worsted Weight Brushed Acrylic Yarn:
46 ounces, (1,310 grams, 2,330 yards)
Crochet hook, size G (4.00 mm) **or** size needed for gauge

GAUGE: Each Square = 15"

Gauge Swatch: 2³/₄" square
Work same as Square through Rnd 2.

STITCH GUIDE

> **POPCORN**
> 4 Dc in st or sp indicated, drop loop from hook, insert hook in first dc of 4-dc group, hook dropped loop and draw through (*Fig. 14, page 140*).

SQUARE (Make 12)
Ch 6; join with slip st to form a ring.
Rnd 1 (Right side)**:** Ch 3 **(counts as first dc, now and throughout)**, 2 dc in ring, (ch 3, 3 dc in ring) 3 times, ch 2, sc in first dc to form last ch-3 sp: 12 dc and 4 ch-3 sps.
Note: Loop a short piece of yarn around any stitch to mark Rnd 1 as **right** side.
Rnd 2: Ch 3, dc in last ch-3 sp made and in next 3 dc, (2 dc, ch 3, dc) in next ch-3 sp, ch 1, dc in next dc, work Popcorn in next dc, dc in next dc, ch 1, (dc, ch 3, dc) in next ch-3 sp, ch 1, dc in next dc, ch 1, skip next dc, dc in next dc, ch 1, (dc, ch 3, dc) in next ch-3 sp, ch 1, dc in next dc, work Popcorn in next dc, dc in next dc, ch 1, dc in same sp as first dc, ch 2, sc in first dc to form last ch-3 sp: 19 dc, 2 Popcorns, and 11 sps.

Rnd 3: Ch 3, dc in last ch-3 sp made and in next dc, ch 1, skip next 2 dc, (dc, ch 3, dc) in next dc, ch 1, skip next 2 dc, dc in next dc, (2 dc, ch 3, dc) in next ch-3 sp, † ch 1, dc in next dc, work Popcorn in next ch-1 sp, dc in next dc, ch 1, dc in next dc, work Popcorn in next ch-1 sp, dc in next dc, ch 1 †, (dc, ch 3, dc) in next ch-3 sp, ch 1, dc in next dc, skip next ch-1 sp, 5 dc in next ch-1 sp, skip next dc, dc in next dc, ch 1, (dc, ch 3, dc) in next ch-3 sp, repeat from † to † once, dc in same sp as first dc, ch 2, sc in first dc to form last ch-3 sp: 29 dc and 15 sps.
Rnd 4: Ch 3, dc in last ch-3 sp made and in next dc, ch 1, skip next 2 dc, dc in next dc, 9 dc in next ch-3 sp, dc in next dc, ch 1, skip next 2 dc, dc in next dc, (2 dc, ch 3, dc) in next ch-3 sp, ch 1, † dc in next dc, work Popcorn in next ch-1 sp, dc in next dc, ch 1 †; repeat from † to † 2 times **more**, (dc, ch 3, dc) in next ch-3 sp, (ch 1, dc in next dc) twice, skip next 2 dc, 5 dc in next dc, skip next 2 dc, (dc in next dc, ch 1) twice, (dc, ch 3, dc) in next ch-3 sp, ch 1, repeat from † to † 3 times, dc in same sp as first dc, ch 2, sc in first dc to form last ch-3 sp: 44 dc and 18 sps.
Rnd 5: Ch 4 **(counts as first dc plus ch 1, now and throughout)**, dc in next 3 dc, ch 1, hdc in next 5 dc, 2 hdc in next dc, hdc in next 5 dc, ch 1, dc in next 3 dc, ch 1, (dc, ch 3, dc) in next ch-3 sp, ch 1, † dc in next dc, work Popcorn in next ch-1 sp, dc in next dc, ch 1 †; repeat from † to † 3 times **more**, (dc, ch 3, dc) in next ch-3 sp, ch 1, (dc in next dc, ch 1) 3 times, skip next 2 dc, 5 dc in next dc, ch 1, skip next 2 dc, (dc in next dc, ch 1) 3 times, (dc, ch 3, dc) in next ch-3 sp, ch 1, repeat from † to † 4 times, dc in same sp as first dc, ch 2, sc in first dc to form last ch-3 sp: 41 dc and 26 sps.
Rnd 6: Ch 4, dc in next dc, ch 1, dc in next 3 dc, ch 2, skip next 2 hdc, hdc in next 3 hdc, 2 hdc in each of next 2 hdc, hdc in next 3 hdc, ch 2, skip next 2 hdc, dc in next 3 dc, ch 1, dc in next dc, ch 1, (dc, ch 3, dc) in next ch-3 sp, ch 1, † dc in next dc, work Popcorn in next ch-1 sp, dc in next dc, ch 1 †; repeat from † to † 4 times **more**, (dc, ch 3, dc) in next ch-3 sp, ch 1, dc in next dc, skip next ch-1 sp, 5 dc in next ch-1 sp, ch 1, skip next 4 dc, 5 dc in next dc, ch 1, skip next 2 ch-1 sps, 5 dc in next ch-1 sp, skip next dc, dc in next dc, ch 1, (dc, ch 3, dc) in next ch-3 sp, ch 1, repeat from † to † 5 times, dc in same sp as first dc, ch 2, sc in first dc to form last ch-3 sp: 53 dc and 26 sps.

Continued on page 114.

Rnd 7: Ch 4, (dc in next dc, ch 1) 3 times, skip next dc, dc in next dc, 2 dc in next ch-2 sp, ch 2, skip next 2 hdc, sc in next 6 hdc, ch 2, 2 dc in next ch-2 sp, dc in next dc, ch 1, skip next dc, (dc in next dc, ch 1) 3 times, (dc, ch 3, dc) in next ch-3 sp, ch 1, † dc in next dc, work Popcorn in next ch-1 sp, dc in next dc, ch 1 †; repeat from † to † 5 times **more**, (dc, ch 3, dc) in next ch-3 sp, (ch 1, dc in next dc) twice, skip next 2 dc, 5 dc in next dc, ★ ch 1, skip next 4 dc, 5 dc in next dc; repeat from ★ once **more**, skip next 2 dc, (dc in next dc, ch 1) twice, (dc, ch 3, dc) in next ch-3 sp, ch 1, repeat from † to † 6 times, dc in same sp as first dc, ch 2, sc in first dc to form last ch-3 sp: 63 dc and 34 sps.

Rnd 8: Ch 4, (dc in next dc, ch 1) 5 times, skip next dc, dc in next dc, 2 dc in next ch-2 sp, ch 2, skip next 2 sc, sc in next 2 sc, ch 2, 2 dc in next ch-2 sp, dc in next dc, ch 1, skip next dc, (dc in next dc, ch 1) 5 times, (dc, ch 3, dc) in next ch-3 sp, ch 1, † dc in next dc, work Popcorn in next ch-1 sp, dc in next dc, ch 1 †; repeat from † to † 6 times **more**, (dc, ch 3, dc) in next ch-3 sp, ch 1, (dc in next dc, ch 1) 3 times, skip next 2 dc, 5 dc in next dc, ch 1, ★ skip next 4 dc, 5 dc in next dc, ch 1; repeat from ★ once **more**, skip next 2 dc, (dc in next dc, ch 1) 3 times, (dc, ch 3, dc) in next ch-3 sp, ch 1, repeat from † to † 7 times, dc in same sp as first dc, ch 2, sc in first dc to form last ch-3 sp: 73 dc and 44 sps.

Rnd 9: Ch 4, (dc in next dc, ch 1) 7 times, skip next dc, dc in next dc, 2 dc in next ch-2 sp, ch 1, 2 dc in next ch-2 sp, dc in next dc, ch 1, skip next dc, (dc in next dc, ch 1) 7 times, (dc, ch 3, dc) in next ch-3 sp, ch 1, (dc in next dc, ch 1) 16 times, (dc, ch 3, dc) in next ch-3 sp, ch 1, dc in next dc, skip next ch-1 sp, 5 dc in next ch-1 sp, ch 1, ★ skip next 4 dc, 5 dc in next dc, ch 1; repeat from ★ 2 times **more**, skip next 2 ch-1 sps, 5 dc in next ch-1 sp, skip next dc, dc in next dc, ch 1, (dc, ch 3, dc) in next ch-3 sp, ch 1, (dc in next dc, ch 1) 16 times, dc in same sp as first dc, ch 2, sc in first dc to form last ch-3 sp: 87 dc and 61 sps.

Rnd 10: Ch 3, (dc in next dc, ch 1) 9 times, skip next dc, (dc in next dc, ch 1) twice, skip next dc, dc in next dc, (ch 1, dc in next dc) 8 times, (dc, ch 3, dc) in next ch-3 sp, ch 1, (dc in next dc, ch 1) 18 times, (dc, ch 3, dc) in next ch-3 sp, ch 1, (dc in next dc, ch 1) twice, skip next 2 dc, 5 dc in next dc, ch 1, ★ skip next 4 dc, 5 dc in next dc, ch 1; repeat from ★ 3 times **more**, skip next 2 dc, (dc in next dc, ch 1) twice, (dc, ch 3, dc) in next ch-3 sp, ch 1, (dc in next dc, ch 1) 18 times, dc in same sp as first dc, ch 2, sc in first dc to form last ch-3 sp: 93 dc and 71 sps.

Rnd 11: Ch 4, skip next dc, dc in next dc, (dc in next ch-1 sp and in next dc) 19 times, ch 1, skip next dc, (dc, ch 3, dc) in next ch-3 sp, ch 1, dc in next dc, (dc in next ch-1 sp and in next dc) 19 times, ch 1, (dc, ch 3, dc) in next ch-3 sp, ch 1, (dc in next dc, ch 1) 3 times, skip next 2 dc, 5 dc in next dc, ch 1, ★ skip next 4 dc, 5 dc in next dc, ch 1; repeat from ★ 3 times **more**, skip next 2 dc, (dc in next dc, ch 1) 3 times, (dc, ch 3, dc) in next ch-3 sp, ch 1, dc in next dc, (dc in next ch-1 sp and in next dc) 19 times, ch 1, dc in same sp as first dc, ch 2, sc in first dc to form last ch-3 sp: 156 dc and 22 sps.

Rnd 12: Ch 4, dc in next dc and in each ch-1 sp and each dc across to next ch-3 sp, ch 1, (dc, ch 3, dc) in ch-3 sp, ch 1, dc in each dc and in each ch-1 sp across to next ch-3 sp, ch 1, (dc, ch 3, dc) in ch-3 sp, ch 1, (dc in next dc, ch 1) 4 times, skip next 2 dc, 5 dc in next dc, ch 1, ★ skip next 4 dc, 5 dc in next dc, ch 1; repeat from ★ 3 times **more**, skip next 2 dc, (dc in next dc, ch 1) 4 times, (dc, ch 3, dc) in next ch-3 sp, ch 1, dc in each dc and in each ch-1 sp across, ch 1, dc in same sp as first dc, ch 2, sc in first dc to form last ch-3 sp: 170 dc and 24 sps.

Rnd 13: Ch 4, dc in next dc and in each ch-1 sp and each dc across to next ch-3 sp, ch 1, (dc, ch 3, dc) in ch-3 sp, ch 1, dc in next dc and in each ch-1 sp and each dc across to next ch-3 sp, ch 1, (dc, ch 3, dc) in next ch-3 sp, (ch 1, dc in next dc) 5 times, ch 2, skip next 2 dc, slip st in next dc, ch 2, ★ sc in next ch-1 sp, ch 2, skip next 2 dc, slip st in next dc, ch 2; repeat from ★ 3 times **more**, skip next 2 dc, (dc in next dc, ch 1) 5 times, (dc, ch 3, dc) in next ch-3 sp, ch 1, dc in each dc and in each ch-1 sp across, ch 1, dc in same sp as first dc, ch 2, sc in first dc to form last ch-3 sp: 159 dc and 30 sps.

Rnd 14: Ch 4, † (dc in next dc, ch 1) twice, (skip next st, dc in next dc, ch 1) across to next ch-3 sp, (dc, ch 3, dc) in ch-3 sp, ch 1 †; repeat from † to † once **more**, (dc in next dc, ch 1) 6 times, place marker around last dc made to mark bottom edge, skip next ch, dc in next ch, ch 1, skip next slip st, dc in next ch, ch 1, skip next ch, ★ dc in next sc, ch 1, skip next ch, dc in next ch, ch 1, skip next slip st, dc in next ch, ch 1, skip next ch; repeat from ★ 3 times **more**, (dc in next dc, ch 1) 6 times, (dc, ch 3, dc) in next ch-3 sp, ch 1, (dc in next dc, ch 1) twice, (skip next st, dc in next dc, ch 1) across, dc in same sp as first dc, ch 3; join with slip st to first dc, finish off: 112 dc and 112 sps.

ASSEMBLY

Assemble Afghan by forming 3 vertical strips of 4 Squares each. Join Squares as follows:
With **right** sides together, match sps on bottom edge of one Square to top edge of next Square. Working through both thicknesses, join yarn with slip st in first corner ch-3 sp; (ch 1, slip st in next sp) across; finish off.
Join strips together in same manner.

EDGING

With **right** side facing, join yarn with slip st in any st; working from **left** to **right**, work reverse sc in each dc and in each ch-1 sp around working 3 reverse sc in each corner ch-3 sp *(Figs. 15a-d, page 140)*; join with slip st to first st, finish off.

Chill Chaser

Chase away winter chills with a hearty, texture-rich cover-up. The flickering stripes of red and white mimic the hot-and-cold contrast of fire and ice.

Finished Size: 46" x 68"

MATERIALS

Worsted Weight Yarn:
    Grey - 43 ounces, (1,220 grams, 2,950 yards)
    Red - $10^1/_4$ ounces, (290 grams, 700 yards)
    White - $7^1/_2$ ounces, (210 grams, 515 yards)
Crochet hook, size H (5.00 mm) **or** size needed for gauge
Yarn needle

GAUGE: In pattern, 16 sc and Rows 1-7 = 4"
        First Panel = $6^1/_8$"w
        Center Panel = $8^1/_2$"w
        Last Panel = $5^3/_4$"w

Gauge Swatch: 4" square
Ch 17 **loosely**.
Work same as First Panel for 7 rows.
Finish off.

STITCH GUIDE

FRONT POST TREBLE CROCHET
    (abbreviated FPtr)
YO twice, insert hook from **front** to **back** around post of st indicated *(Fig. 10, page 139)*, YO and pull up a loop even with loop on hook (4 loops on hook), (YO and draw through 2 loops on hook) 3 times.

BACK POST TREBLE CROCHET
    (abbreviated BPtr)
YO twice, insert hook from **back** to **front** around post of st indicated *(Fig. 10, page 139)*, YO and pull up a loop even with loop on hook (4 loops on hook), (YO and draw through 2 loops on hook) 3 times.

CLUSTER (uses one st)
★ YO, insert hook in st indicated, YO and pull up a loop, YO and draw through 2 loops on hook; repeat from ★ 2 times **more**, YO and draw through all 4 loops on hook *(Figs. 11a & b, page 139)*.

Note: Each row is worked across length of Afghan.

FIRST PANEL

With Grey, ch 269 **loosely**.
Row 1: Sc in second ch from hook and in each ch across: 268 sc.
Row 2 (Right side): Ch 3 **(counts as first dc, now and throughout)**, turn; dc in next sc, ★ skip next 2 sc, tr in next sc, ch 1, working **behind** tr just made, tr in first skipped sc; repeat from ★ across to last 2 sc, dc in last 2 sc: 180 sts and 88 ch-1 sps.
*Note: Loop a short piece of yarn around first tr made to mark Row 2 as **right** side and bottom edge.*

Continued on page 116.

Row 3: Ch 3, turn; skip next dc, work BPtr around next tr, ch 1, working in **front** of BPtr just made, tr in sp **before** skipped dc *(Fig. 20, page 141)*, ★ skip next tr, work BPtr around next tr, ch 1, working in **front** of BPtr just made, work BPtr around skipped tr; repeat from ★ across to last ch-1 sp, skip next tr and next dc, tr in sp **before** last dc, ch 1, working in **front** of tr just made, work BPtr around skipped tr, dc in last dc: 180 sts and 89 ch-1 sps.

Row 4: Ch 3, turn; dc in next BPtr, skip next tr, work FPtr around next BPtr, ch 1, working **behind** FPtr just made, work FPtr around skipped tr, ★ skip next BPtr, work FPtr around next BPtr, ch 1, working **behind** FPtr just made, work FPtr around skipped BPtr; repeat from ★ across to last 2 BPtr, skip next BPtr, work FPtr around next tr, ch 1, working **behind** FPtr just made, work FPtr around skipped BPtr, dc in next BPtr and in last dc.

Row 5: Ch 3, turn; skip next dc, work BPtr around next FPtr, ch 1, working in **front** of BPtr just made, tr in sp **before** skipped dc, ★ skip next FPtr, work BPtr around next FPtr, ch 1, working in **front** of BPtr just made, work BPtr around skipped FPtr; repeat from ★ across to last ch-1 sp, skip next FPtr and next dc, tr in sp **before** last dc, ch 1, working in **front** of tr just made, work BPtr around skipped FPtr, dc in last dc.

Rows 6-8: Repeat Rows 4 and 5 once, then repeat Row 4 once **more**.

Row 9: Ch 1, turn; sc in each st and in each ch-1 sp across; finish off: 268 sc.

Row 10: With **right** side facing, join White with sc in first sc *(see Joining With Sc, page 140)*; sc in next sc and in each sc across.

Row 11: Ch 1, turn; sc in first sc, ★ ch 2, skip next 2 sc, sc in next sc; repeat from ★ across; finish off: 90 sc and 89 ch-2 sps.

Row 12: With **right** side facing, join Red with sc in first sc; ★ working **behind** next ch-2 *(Fig. 18, page 141)*, dc in 2 skipped sc one row **below** ch-2, sc in next sc; repeat from ★ across; finish off: 268 sts.

Row 13: With **right** side facing, join Grey with sc in first sc; (sc in next 2 dc, work Cluster in next sc) across to last 3 sts, sc in last 3 sts; finish off: 180 sc and 88 Clusters.

Row 14: With **right** side facing, join White with sc in first sc; ch 2, ★ skip next 2 sc, sc in next Cluster, ch 2; repeat from ★ across to last 3 sc, skip next 2 sc, sc in last sc; finish off: 90 sc and 89 ch-2 sps.

Rows 15 and 16: Repeat Rows 12 and 13.

CENTER 4 PANELS
Work same as First Panel.

TRIM
Row 1: With **right** facing and working in free loops of beginning ch *(Fig. 17b, page 141)*, join White with sc in ch at base of first sc; sc in next ch and in each ch across: 268 sc.

Row 2: Ch 1, turn; sc in first sc, ★ ch 2, skip next 2 sc, sc in next sc; repeat from ★ across; finish off: 90 sc and 89 ch-2 sps.

Row 3: With **right** side facing, join Red with sc in first sc; ★ working **behind** next ch-2, dc in 2 skipped sc one row **below** ch-2, sc in next sc; repeat from ★ across; finish off: 268 sts.

Row 4: With **right** side facing, join Grey with sc in first sc; (sc in next 2 dc, work Cluster in next sc) across to last 3 sts, sc in last 3 sts; finish off: 180 sc and 88 Clusters.

Row 5: With **right** side facing, join White with sc in first sc; ch 2, ★ skip next 2 sc, sc in next Cluster, ch 2; repeat from ★ across to last 3 sc, skip next 2 sc, sc in last sc; finish off: 90 sc and 89 ch-2 sps.

Row 6: With **right** side facing, join Red with sc in first sc; ★ working **behind** next ch-2, dc in 2 skipped sc one row **below** ch-2, sc in next sc; repeat from ★ across; finish off: 268 sts.

LAST PANEL
Work same as First Panel through Row 9.

TRIM
Work same as Trim on Center 4 Panels.

ASSEMBLY
With Grey, holding Panels with bottom edges at same end, matching sts and working through both loops, whipstitch Panels together beginning in first sc and ending in last sc *(Fig. 21b, page 142)*.

EDGING
Rnd 1: With **right** side facing, join White with sc in last sc on Last Panel in upper right corner; 2 sc in same st, sc evenly across end of rows; working in free loops of beginning ch on First Panel, 3 sc in ch at base of first sc, sc in next ch and in each ch across to last ch, 3 sc in last ch; sc evenly across end of rows; working in sts across Row 9 of Last Panel, 3 sc in first sc, sc in next sc and in each sc across; join with slip st to first sc.

Rnd 2: Working from **left** to **right**, work reverse sc in each sc around *(Figs. 15a-d, page 140)*; join with slip st to first st, finish off.

Tradition

Fisherman afghans are traditionally known to provide unsurpassable warmth, and our fringed version is no exception. You'll reel in the compliments with this catch of the day!

Finished Size: 47" x 63"

MATERIALS

Worsted Weight Yarn:
  64 ounces, (1,820 grams, 3,615 yards)
  Crochet hook, size I (5.50 mm) **or** size needed for gauge

GAUGE: (Cable, 10 dc, Cable) = $5^1/_2$";
  9 rows = 4"

STITCH GUIDE

FRONT POST DOUBLE CROCHET
  (abbreviated FPdc)
YO, insert hook from **front** to **back** around post of st indicated *(Fig. 10, page 139)*, YO and pull up a loop (3 loops on hook), (YO and draw through 2 loops on hook) twice. Skip st behind FPdc.

BACK POST DOUBLE CROCHET
  (abbreviated BPdc)
YO, insert hook from **back** to **front** around post of st indicated *(Fig. 10, page 139)*, YO and pull up a loop (3 loops on hook), (YO and draw through 2 loops on hook) twice. Skip st in front of BPdc.

FRONT POST TREBLE CROCHET
  (abbreviated FPtr)
YO twice, insert hook from **front** to **back** around post of st indicated *(Fig. 10, page 139)*, YO and pull up a loop (4 loops on hook), (YO and draw through 2 loops on hook) 3 times. Skip st behind FPtr.

POPCORN
4 Dc in st indicated, drop loop from hook, insert hook in first dc of 4-dc group, hook dropped loop and draw through st *(Fig. 14, page 140)*, ch 1 to close.

CABLE (uses next 4 sts)
Skip next st, work FPdc around each of next 3 sts, working in **front** of last 3 FPdc made, work FPtr around skipped st.

AFGHAN

Ch 153 **loosely.**

Row 1: Dc in fourth ch from hook **(3 skipped chs count as first dc)** and in each ch across: 151 dc.

Row 2 (Right side): Ch 3 **(counts as first dc, now and throughout)**, turn; dc in next 2 dc, † work FPdc around next dc, work BPdc around next dc, work Popcorn in next dc, work BPdc around next dc, work FPdc around next dc, dc in next 3 dc †, work Cable, dc in next 10 dc, work Cable, dc in next 3 dc, ★ work BPdc around next dc, work Popcorn in next dc, work BPdc around each of next 2 dc, skip next 2 dc, 5 dc in next dc, skip next 2 dc, work BPdc around each of next 2 dc, work Popcorn in next dc, work BPdc around next dc, dc in next 3 dc, work Cable, dc in next 10 dc, work Cable, dc in next 3 dc; repeat from ★ 2 times **more**, then repeat from † to † once: 8 Cables, 8 Popcorns, and 85 dc.

Row 3: Ch 2 **(counts as first hdc)**, turn; hdc in next 2 dc, † work BPdc around next FPdc, work FPdc around next BPdc, hdc in next Popcorn, work FPdc around next BPdc, work BPdc around next FPdc, hdc in next 3 dc †, work BPdc around each of next 4 sts, hdc in next 10 dc, work BPdc around each of next 4 sts, hdc in next 3 dc, ★ work FPdc around next BPdc, hdc in next Popcorn, work FPdc around each of next 2 BPdc, skip next dc, work 2 BPdc around next dc, sc in next dc, work 2 BPdc around next dc, skip next dc, work FPdc around each of next 2 BPdc, hdc in next Popcorn, work FPdc around next BPdc, hdc in next 3 dc, work BPdc around each of next 4 sts, hdc in next 10 dc, work BPdc around each of next 4 sts, hdc in next 3 dc; repeat from ★ 2 times **more**, then repeat from † to † once.

Row 4: Ch 3, turn; dc in next 2 hdc, † work FPdc around next BPdc, work BPdc around next FPdc, work Popcorn in next hdc, work BPdc around next FPdc, work FPdc around next BPdc, dc in next 3 hdc †, work Cable, dc in next 10 hdc, work Cable, dc in next 3 hdc, ★ work BPdc around next FPdc, work Popcorn in next hdc, work BPdc around each of next 2 FPdc, skip next 2 BPdc, 5 dc in next sc, skip next 2 BPdc, work BPdc around each of next 2 FPdc, work Popcorn in next hdc, work BPdc around next FPdc, dc in next 3 hdc, work Cable, dc in next 10 hdc, work Cable, dc in next 3 hdc; repeat from ★ 2 times **more**, then repeat from † to † once: 8 Cables, 8 Popcorns and 85 dc.

Repeat Rows 3 and 4 until Afghan measures approximately 63" from beginning ch, ending by working Row 4; finish off.

Holding 6 strands of yarn together, each 16" long, add fringe across short edges of Afghan *(Figs. 22a & c, page 142)*.

Pretty Poinsettias

Crocheted in squares, this afghan showcases the poinsettia's rich red coloring.
The Christmasy cover will add cozy cheer to your Yuletide décor.

Finished Size: 50" x 68"

MATERIALS
Worsted Weight Yarn:
   Ecru - 33 ounces, (940 grams, 1,865 yards)
   Green - 19 ounces, (540 grams, 1,075 yards)
   Red - 15 ounces, (430 grams, 850 yards)
Crochet hook, size J (6.00 mm) **or** size needed for gauge

GAUGE: Each Square = 9"

Gauge Swatch: 5$\frac{1}{4}$" square
Work same as Square through Rnd 5.

STITCH GUIDE

BEGINNING POPCORN
Ch 3 **(counts as first dc)**, 3 dc in ring, drop loop from hook, insert hook in first dc of 4-dc group, hook dropped loop and draw through *(Fig. 14, page 140)*.

POPCORN
4 Dc in st or sp indicated, drop loop from hook, insert hook in first dc of 4-dc group, hook dropped loop and draw through *(Fig. 14, page 140)*.

FRONT POST DOUBLE CROCHET
   (abbreviated FPdc)
YO, insert hook from **front** to **back** around post of st indicated *(Fig. 10, page 139)*, YO and pull up a loop even with last st made (3 loops on hook), (YO and draw through 2 loops on hook) twice.

BACK POST DOUBLE CROCHET
   (abbreviated BPdc)
YO, insert hook from **back** to **front** around post of st indicated *(Fig. 10, page 139)*, YO and pull up a loop even with last st made (3 loops on hook), (YO and draw through 2 loops on hook) twice.

FRONT POST TREBLE CROCHET
   (abbreviated FPtr)
YO twice, insert hook from **front** to **back** around post of st indicated *(Fig. 10, page 139)*, YO and pull up a loop even with last st made (4 loops on hook), (YO and draw through 2 loops on hook) 3 times.

LONG SINGLE CROCHET
   (abbreviated LSC)
Working **around** previous row, insert hook in sc one rnd **below** next sc, YO and pull up a loop even with last sc made, YO and draw though both loops on hook *(Fig. 9, page 139)*.

SQUARE (Make 35)

With Red, ch 4; join with slip st to form a ring.

Rnd 1 (Right side): Work Beginning Popcorn, ch 3, (work Popcorn in ring, ch 3) 3 times; join with slip st to top of Beginning Popcorn, finish off: 4 Popcorns and 4 ch-3 sps.

Note: Loop a short piece of yarn around any stitch to mark Rnd 1 as **right** side.

Rnd 2: With **right** side facing, join Green with dc in first ch-3 sp *(see Joining With Dc, page 140)*; (2 dc, ch 2, 3 dc) in same sp, ch 2, (3 dc, ch 2) twice in each ch-3 sp around; join with slip st to first dc, finish off: 8 ch-2 sps.

Rnd 3: With **right** side facing, join Ecru with sc in ch-2 sp before joining *(see Joining With Sc, page 140)*; 4 sc in same sp, 5 sc in each ch-2 sp around; join with slip st to first sc, finish off: 40 sc.

Rnd 4: With **right** side facing, join Red with dc in center sc of first 5-sc group; (2 dc, ch 2, 3 dc) in same st, ch 2, (work FPdc around center dc of **next** 3-dc group on Rnd 2, ch 2) twice, skip next 5-sc group on Rnd 3 (behind FPdc just made), ★ (3 dc, ch 2) twice in center sc of next 5-sc group, (work FPdc around center dc of **next** 3-dc group on Rnd 2, ch 2) twice, skip next 5-sc group on Rnd 3 (behind FPdc just made); repeat from ★ 2 times **more**; join with slip st to first dc, finish off: 32 sts and 16 ch-2 sps.

Rnd 5: With **right** side facing, join Green with sc in any corner ch-2 sp; 4 sc in same sp, ★ † ch 1, skip next dc, sc in next dc, ch 1, skip next dc, sc in next ch, ch 1, skip next ch, sc in next FPdc, ch 1, skip next ch, sc in next ch, ch 1, skip next FPdc, sc in next ch, ch 1, skip next ch, sc in next dc, ch 1, skip next dc, sc in next dc, ch 1 †, 5 sc in next corner ch-2 sp; repeat from ★ 2 times **more**, then repeat from † to † once; join with slip st to first sc, finish off: 48 sc and 32 ch-1 sps.

Continued on page 122.

Rnd 6: With **right** side facing, join Ecru with dc in center sc of any corner 5-sc group; 2 dc in same st, ★ † skip next sc, dc in next sc, (ch 1, dc in next sc) 8 times, skip next sc †, (3 dc, ch 2, 3 dc) in next sc; repeat from ★ 2 times **more**, then repeat from † to † once, 3 dc in same st as first dc, hdc in first dc to form last ch-2 sp; do **not** finish off: 60 dc and 36 sps.

Rnd 7: Ch 3 **(counts as first dc, now and throughout)**, (2 dc, ch 2, 3 dc) in last ch-2 sp made, ★ † skip next 3 dc, work FPdc around next dc, (work Popcorn in next dc, ch 1, work FPdc around next dc) 4 times, skip next 3 dc †, (3 dc, ch 2, 3 dc) in next corner ch-2 sp; repeat from ★ 2 times **more**, then repeat from † to † once; join with slip st to first dc, finish off: 16 Popcorns, 20 FPdc, and 20 sps.

Rnd 8: With **right** side facing, join Green with sc in any corner ch-2 sp; 2 sc in same sp, ★ † sc in next 2 dc, work FPtr around first dc of next 3-dc group on Rnd 6, skip next dc on Rnd 7, (sc in next 2 sts and in next ch) 4 times, sc in next FPdc, work FPtr around third dc of next 3-dc group on Rnd 6, skip next dc on Rnd 7, sc in next 2 dc †, 3 sc in next corner ch-2 sp; repeat from ★ 2 times **more**, then repeat from † to † once; join with slip st to first sc, do **not** finish off: 88 sts.

Rnd 9: Ch 1, sc in same st and in each st around working 3 sc in center sc of each corner 3-sc group; join with slip st to first sc, finish off: 96 sc.

Rnd 10: With **right** side facing, join Red with sc in center sc of any corner 3-sc group; 2 sc in same st, ch 1, skip next sc, (work LSC, ch 1, skip next sc) 11 times, ★ 3 sc in next sc, ch 1, skip next sc, (work LSC, ch 1, skip next sc) 11 times; repeat from ★ 2 times **more**; join with slip st to first sc, finish off: 56 sts and 48 ch-1 sps.

Rnd 11: With **right** side facing, join Ecru with dc in center sc of any corner 3-sc group; (dc, ch 2, 2 dc) in same st, dc in next ch-1 sp, (ch 1, dc in next ch-1 sp) 11 times, skip next sc, ★ (2 dc, ch 2, 2 dc) in next sc, dc in next ch-1 sp, (ch 1, dc in next ch-1 sp) 11 times, skip next sc; repeat from ★ 2 times **more**; join with slip st to first dc, finish off: 64 dc and 48 sps.

ASSEMBLY

Join Squares together forming 5 vertical strips of 7 Squares each as follows:

Holding 2 Squares with **right** sides together and working through **both** thicknesses, join Ecru with sc in first corner ch-2 sp; sc in next 2 dc, ch 1, (sc in next ch-1 sp, ch 1) 11 times, skip next dc, sc in next 2 dc and in corner ch-2 sp; finish off.

Join strips together in same manner.

EDGING

Rnd 1: With **wrong** side facing, join Ecru with dc in any corner ch-2 sp; 2 dc in same sp, ★ † skip next 2 dc, 2 dc in each of next 12 dc, (skip next dc, 2 dc in next dc, skip next joining, 2 dc in next dc, skip next dc, 2 dc in each of next 12 dc) across to within 2 dc of next corner ch-2 sp, skip next 2 dc †, (3 dc, ch 2, 3 dc) in corner ch-2 sp; repeat from ★ 2 times **more**, then repeat from † to † once, 3 dc in same sp as first dc, ch 2; join with slip st to first dc: 680 dc and 4 ch-2 sps.

Rnd 2: Turn; (slip st, ch 3, 2 dc, ch 2, 3 dc) in first corner ch-2 sp, skip next 3 dc, dc in next dc and in each dc across to within 3 dc of next corner ch-2 sp, skip next 3 dc, ★ (3 dc, ch 2, 3 dc) in corner ch-2 sp, skip next 3 dc, dc in next dc and in each dc across to within 3 dc of next corner ch-2 sp, skip next 3 dc; repeat from ★ 2 times **more**; join with slip st to first dc, finish off.

Rnd 3: With **right** side facing, join Green with sc in any corner ch-2 sp; 2 sc in same sp, ★ † sc in next 3 dc, (work FPdc around next dc, work BPdc around next dc) across to within 3 dc of next corner ch-2 sp, sc in next 3 dc †, 3 sc in corner ch-2 sp; repeat from ★ 2 times **more**, then repeat from † to † once; join with slip st to first sc, finish off.

Rnd 4: With **wrong** side facing and working across short edge of Afghan, join Red with dc in center sc of first corner 3-sc group; (2 dc, ch 2, 3 dc) in same st, † [skip next 2 sc, (dc, ch 3, sc in third ch from hook, dc) in next st] across to within 2 sc of next corner 3-sc group, skip next 3 sc, (3 dc, ch 2, 3 dc) in next corner sc, [skip next 2 sc, (dc, ch 3, sc in third ch from hook, dc) in next st] across to within one sc of next corner 3-sc group, skip next 2 sc †, (3 dc, ch 2, 3 dc) in next corner sc, repeat from † to † once; join with slip st to first dc, finish off.

Icicles

Capture the essence of winter with an afghan that lends an air of seasonal excitement.
Extended clusters create the enchanting appearance of icicles hanging from the eaves.

Finished Size: 51" x 71"

MATERIALS

Worsted Weight Yarn:
Aran - 34 ounces, (970 grams, 2,330 yards)
Dk Blue - 10 ounces, (280 grams, 685 yards)
Blue - 10 ounces, (280 grams, 685 yards)
Lt Blue - 8^1/$_2$ ounces, (240 grams, 585 yards)
Black - 8^1/$_2$ ounces, (240 grams, 585 yards)
Crochet hook, size J (6.00 mm) **or** size needed for
gauge

GAUGE: In pattern, 12 sts and 16 rows = 4"

Gauge Swatch: 5"w x 3^3/$_4$"h
With Aran, ch 16 **loosely**.
Work same as Afghan Body for 15 rows.

STITCH GUIDE

CLUSTER
Working **around** previous rows, pull up a loop
in sc one row **below** next sc **and** in sc two rows
below same sc *(Fig. 1a)*, pull up a loop in sc one
row **below** next sc *(Fig. 1b)*, YO and draw
through 3 loops on hook, YO and draw through
remaining 2 loops on hook. Skip sc behind
Cluster.

Fig. 1a   **Fig. 1b**

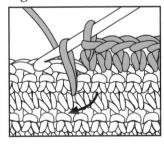   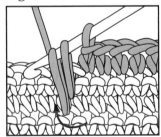

V-ST
(Dc, ch 1, dc) in st indicated.
PICOT
Ch 3, sc in third ch from hook.

AFGHAN BODY

With Aran, ch 140 **loosely**.
Row 1: Sc in second ch from hook and in each ch
across: 139 sc.
Row 2 (Right side): Ch 1, turn; sc in each sc across.
Note: Loop a short piece of yarn around any stitch
to mark Row 2 as **right** side.
Row 3: Ch 1, turn; sc in each sc across; finish off.
Row 4: With **right** side facing, join Black with sc in
first sc *(see Joining With Sc, page 140)*; sc in next
2 sc, (work Cluster, sc in next 3 sc) across: 105 sc and
34 Clusters.
Row 5: Ch 1, turn; sc in each st across; finish off:
139 sc.
Row 6: With **right** side facing, join Dk Blue with sc
in first sc; work Cluster, (sc in next 3 sc, work
Cluster) across to last sc, sc in last sc: 104 sc and
35 Clusters.
Row 7: Ch 1, turn; sc in each st across; finish off:
139 sc.
Row 8: With **right** side facing, join Blue with sc in
first sc; sc in next 2 sc, (work Cluster, sc in next 3 sc)
across: 105 sc and 34 Clusters.
Row 9: Ch 1, turn; sc in each st across; finish off:
139 sc.
Row 10: With **right** side facing, join Lt Blue with sc
in first sc; work Cluster, (sc in next 3 sc, work
Cluster) across to last sc, sc in last sc: 104 sc and
35 Clusters.
Row 11: Ch 1, turn; sc in each st across; finish off:
139 sc.
Row 12: With **right** side facing, join Aran with sc in
first sc; sc in next 2 sc, (work Cluster, sc in next 3 sc)
across: 105 sc and 34 Clusters.
Rows 13-15: Ch 1, turn; sc in each st across; at end of
last row, finish off: 139 sc.
Row 16: With **right** side facing, join Lt Blue with sc
in first sc; work Cluster, (sc in next 3 sc, work
Cluster) across to last sc, sc in last sc: 104 sc and
35 Clusters.

Continued on page 124.

Row 17: Ch 1, turn; sc in each st across; finish off: 139 sc.

Row 18: With **right** side facing, join Blue with sc in first sc; sc in next 2 sc, (work Cluster, sc in next 3 sc) across: 105 sc and 34 Clusters.

Row 19: Ch 1, turn; sc in each st across; finish off: 139 sc.

Row 20: With **right** side facing, join Dk Blue with sc in first sc; work Cluster, (sc in next 3 sc, work Cluster) across to last sc, sc in last sc: 104 sc and 35 Clusters.

Row 21: Ch 1, turn; sc in each st across; finish off: 139 sc.

Row 22: With **right** side facing, join Black with sc in first sc; sc in next 2 sc, (work Cluster, sc in next 3 sc) across: 105 sc and 34 Clusters.

Row 23: Ch 1, turn; sc in each st across; finish off: 139 sc.

Row 24: With **right** side facing, join Aran with sc in first sc; work Cluster, (sc in next 3 sc, work Cluster) across to last sc, sc in last sc: 104 sc and 35 Clusters.

Rows 25-37: Ch 1, turn; sc in each st across; at end of last row, finish off: 139 sc.

Rows 38-264: Repeat Rows 4-37, 6 times; then repeat Rows 4-26 once **more**.

Finish off.

EDGING

Rnd 1: With **right** side facing, join Aran with slip st in first sc on Row 264; ch 4 **(counts as first dc plus ch 1, now and throughout)**, (dc, work V-St) in same st, skip next 2 sc, (work V-St in next sc, skip next 2 sc) across to last sc, work 3 V-Sts in last sc; working in end of rows, skip first 2 rows, work V-St in next row, (skip next 2 rows, work V-St in next row) across to last 3 rows, skip last 3 rows; working in free loops of beginning ch (*Fig. 17b, page 141*), work 3 V-Sts in ch at base of first sc, skip next 2 chs, (work V-St in next ch, skip next 2 chs) across to last ch, work 3 V-Sts in last ch; working in end of rows, skip first 3 rows, (work V-St in next row, skip next 2 rows) across, work V-St in same st as joining; join with slip st to first dc, finish off: 276 V-Sts.

Rnd 2: With **right** side facing, join Blue with sc in first ch after joining; sc in each dc and in each ch around; join with slip st to first sc, finish off: 828 sc.

Rnd 3: With **right** side facing, join Aran with slip st in same st as joining; ch 4, (dc, work 2 V-Sts) in same st, † skip next 2 sc, (work V-St in next sc, skip next 2 sc) 47 times, work 3 V-Sts in next sc, skip next 2 sc, (work V-St in next sc, skip next 2 sc) 89 times †, work 3 V-Sts in next sc, repeat from † to † once; join with slip st to first dc, do **not** finish off: 284 V-Sts.

Rnd 4: Slip st in next ch-1 sp, ch 1, **turn**; sc in same sp, 5 dc in next ch-1 sp, (sc in next ch-1 sp, 5 dc in next ch-1 sp) around; join with slip st to first sc, finish off.

Rnd 5: With **right** side facing, join Dk Blue with sc in first dc of any 5-dc group; (sc in next dc, work Picot) twice, sc in next 2 dc, skip next sc, ★ sc in next 2 dc, work Picot, sc in next dc, work Picot, sc in next 2 dc, skip next sc; repeat from ★ around; join with slip st to first sc, finish off.

Fireside Companion

Stoke the fire in the hearth and then reach for this toasty throw before settling in with a good book. The warm hues will offer a welcome spot of color on a winter day.

Finished Size: 51" x 69"

MATERIALS
Worsted Weight Yarn:
  Tan - 15 ounces, (430 grams, 850 yards)
  Black - 12 ounces, (340 grams, 680 yards)
  Brown - 12 ounces, (340 grams, 680 yards)
  Lt Green - 11 ounces, (310 grams, 620 yards)
  Dk Green - 5 ounces, (140 grams, 285 yards)
Crochet hook, size I (5.50 mm) **or** size needed for gauge
Yarn needle

GAUGE: In pattern, one repeat = 3"
        Each Strip = 10" wide

Gauge Swatch: $6^1/_4$"w x 5"h
With Lt Green, ch 22.
Work same as First Side.

STITCH GUIDE

> **DECREASE** (uses next 3 sc)
> ★ YO, insert hook in **next** sc, YO and pull up a loop, YO and draw through 2 loops on hook; repeat from ★ 2 times **more**, YO and draw through all 4 loops on hook **(counts as one dc)**.
> **ENDING DECREASE** (uses last 2 sc)
> ★ YO, insert hook in **next** sc, YO and pull up a loop, YO and draw through 2 loops on hook; repeat from ★ once **more**, YO and draw through all 3 loops on hook **(counts as one dc)**.

Note: Each row is worked across length of Strip. When joining yarn and finishing off, leave an 8" end to be worked into fringe.

STRIP (Make 5)
FIRST SIDE
With Lt Green, ch 232.
Row 1: Sc in second ch from hook, ch 1, skip next ch, sc in next ch, ch 1, skip next 2 chs, (dc, ch 3, dc) in next ch, ch 1, skip next 2 chs, sc in next ch, ch 1, ★ (skip next ch, sc in next ch, ch 1) twice, skip next 2 chs, (dc, ch 3, dc) in next ch, ch 1, skip next 2 chs, sc in next ch, ch 1; repeat from ★ across to last 2 chs, skip next ch, sc in last ch: 116 sts and 115 sps.

Row 2 (Right side): Ch 1, turn; sc in first sc and in next ch-1 sp, ch 1, skip next sc, dc in next dc, ch 1, (dc, ch 1) 3 times in next ch-3 sp, dc in next dc, ch 1, ★ skip next ch-1 sp, (sc in next ch-1 sp, ch 1) twice, skip next sc, dc in next dc, ch 1, (dc, ch 1) 3 times in next ch-3 sp, dc in next dc, ch 1; repeat from ★ across to last 2 ch-1 sps, skip next ch-1 sp, sc in next ch-1 sp and in last sc; finish off: 163 sts and 160 ch-1 sps.
Note: Loop a short piece of yarn around any stitch to mark Row 2 as **right** side.

Row 3: With **wrong** side facing, join Black with sc in first sc *(see Joining With Sc, page 140)*; ch 1, skip next sc, (sc in next dc, ch 1) 5 times, ★ skip next ch-1 sp, sc in next ch-1 sp, ch 1, skip next sc, (sc in next dc, ch 1) 5 times; repeat from ★ across to last 2 sc, skip next sc, sc in last sc; finish off: 139 sc and 138 ch-1 sps.

Row 4: With **right** side facing, join Dk Green with slip st in first sc; ch 2, (dc in next sc, ch 1) twice, (dc, ch 1) 3 times in next sc, dc in next sc, ch 1, ★ decrease, ch 1, dc in next sc, ch 1, (dc, ch 1) 3 times in next sc, dc in next sc, ch 1; repeat from ★ across to last 2 sc, work ending decrease; finish off.

Row 5: With **wrong** side facing, join Black with sc in first dc; (ch 1, sc in next dc) across; finish off.

Row 6: With **right** side facing, join Tan with slip st in first sc; ch 2, (dc in next sc, ch 1) twice, (dc, ch 1) 3 times in next sc, dc in next sc, ch 1, ★ decrease, ch 1, dc in next sc, ch 1, (dc, ch 1) 3 times in next sc, dc in next sc, ch 1; repeat from ★ across to last 2 sc, work ending decrease; finish off.

Row 7: With **wrong** side facing, join Brown with sc in first dc; (ch 1, sc in next dc) across; finish off.

Row 8: With **right** side facing, join Tan with slip st in first sc; ch 2, (dc in next sc, ch 1) twice, (dc, ch 1) 3 times in next sc, dc in next sc, ch 1, ★ decrease, ch 1, dc in next sc, ch 1, (dc, ch 1) 3 times in next sc, dc in next sc, ch 1; repeat from ★ across to last 2 sc, work ending decrease; finish off.

Row 9: With **wrong** side facing, join Black with sc in first dc; (ch 1, sc in next dc) across; finish off.

Row 10: With **right** side facing, join Brown with slip st in first sc; ch 4 **(counts as first tr)**, dc in next sc, ch 1, hdc in next sc, ch 1, sc in next sc, ch 1, hdc in next sc, ★ ch 2, decrease, ch 2, hdc in next sc, ch 1, sc in next sc, ch 1, hdc in next sc; repeat from ★ across to last 2 sc, ch 1, dc in next sc, tr in last sc; finish off.

Continued on page 128.

SECOND SIDE

Row 1: With **wrong** side facing and working in free loops of beginning ch *(Fig. 17b, page 141)*, join Lt Green with sc in first ch; ch 1, skip next ch, sc in next ch, ch 1, skip next 2 chs, (dc, ch 3, dc) in next ch, ch 1, skip next 2 chs, sc in next ch, ch 1, ★ (skip next ch, sc in next ch, ch 1) twice, skip next 2 chs, (dc, ch 3, dc) in next ch, ch 1, skip next 2 chs, sc in next ch, ch 1; repeat from ★ 21 times **more**, skip next ch, sc in next ch: 116 sts and 115 sps.
Rows 2-10: Work same as First Side.

ASSEMBLY

With Brown and working through both loops, whipstitch Strips together *(Fig. 21b, page 142)*, beginning in first tr and ending in last tr.

TRIM

Row 1: With **wrong** side facing and working across long edge, join Brown with sc in first tr; sc in next dc, ★ ch 1, skip next st, sc in next st; repeat from ★ across to last tr, sc in last tr.
Row 2: Turn; slip st in first sc, ch 1, (slip st in next ch-1 sp, ch 1) across to last 2 sc, skip next sc, slip st in last sc; finish off.
Repeat for Second Side.

Holding 3 strands of corresponding color yarn together, each 17" long, add additional fringe evenly spaced across short edges of Afghan *(Figs. 22b & d, page 142)*.

Christmas Crowns

Adorn your home for the holidays with a quilt-inspired cover-up in Christmas colors. A patchwork of granny squares forms the traditional Four Crowns pattern.

Finished Size: 48" x 69"

MATERIALS
Worsted Weight Yarn:
Lt Green - 21$^{1}/_{2}$ ounces,
 (610 grams, 1,135 yards)
Green - 12 ounces, (340 grams, 635 yards)
White - 12 ounces, (340 grams, 635 yards)
Red - 10 ounces, (280 grams, 530 yards)
Crochet hook, size I (5.50 mm) **or** size needed for gauge
Yarn needle

GAUGE SWATCH: 3" square
Work same as Square A.

Referring to the Key, make the number of Squares specified in the colors indicated.

SQUARE A

With color indicated, ch 4; join with slip st to form a ring.
Rnd 1 (Right side): Ch 3 **(counts as first dc, now and throughout)**, 2 dc in ring, (ch 2, 3 dc in ring) 3 times, hdc in first dc to form last ch-2 sp: 12 dc and 4 ch-2 sps.
Note: Loop a short piece of yarn around any stitch to mark Rnd 1 as **right** side.
Rnd 2: Ch 3, (2 dc, ch 2, 3 dc) in last ch-2 sp made, ch 1, ★ (3 dc, ch 2, 3 dc) in next ch-2 sp, ch 1; repeat from ★ 2 times **more**; join with slip st to first dc, finish off: 24 dc and 8 sps.

SQUARE B

With first color indicated, ch 4; join with slip st to form a ring.
Rnd 1 (Right side): Ch 5 **(counts as first dc plus ch 2)**, 3 dc in ring, cut first color, with second color indicated, YO and draw through, ch 1, (3 dc, ch 2, 3 dc) in ring, cut second color, with first color, YO and draw through, ch 1, 2 dc in ring; join with slip st to first dc: 12 dc and 4 ch-2 sps.
Note: Mark Rnd 1 as **right** side.

Continued on page 130.

Rnd 2: Slip st in first ch-2 sp, ch 3, (2 dc, ch 2, 3 dc) in same sp, ch 1, 3 dc in next ch-2 sp, cut first color, with second color, YO and draw through, ch 1, 3 dc in same sp, ch 1, (3 dc, ch 2, 3 dc) in next ch-2 sp, ch 1, 3 dc in next ch-2 sp, cut second color, with first color, YO and draw through, ch 1, 3 dc in same sp, ch 1; join with slip st to first dc, finish off: 24 dc and 8 sps.

ASSEMBLY

With matching color, using Placement Diagram as a guide, and working through inside loops only, whipstitch Squares together *(Fig. 21a, page 142)*, forming 15 vertical strips of 22 Squares each; whipstitch strips together in same manner.

PLACEMENT DIAGRAM

EDGING

Rnd 1: With **right** side facing and working across short edge of Afghan, join Lt Green with sc in first corner ch-2 sp *(see Joining With Sc, page 140)*; sc in same sp, sc in each dc and in each sp and joining across to next corner ch-2 sp, ★ 3 sc in corner ch-2 sp, sc in each dc and in each sp and joining across to next corner ch-2 sp; repeat from ★ 2 times **more**, sc in same sp as first sc; join with slip st to first sc: 740 sc.

Rnd 2: Ch 1, 2 sc in same st, ★ † sc in next sc, hdc in next sc, dc in next sc, tr in next sc, dtr in next sc, tr in next sc, dc in next sc, hdc in next sc, sc in next sc, ♥ slip st in next sc, sc in next sc, hdc in next sc, dc in next sc, tr in next sc, dtr in next sc, tr in next sc, dc in next sc, hdc in next sc, sc in next sc ♥, repeat from ♥ to ♥ across to center sc of next corner 3-sc group †, 3 sc in center sc; repeat from ★ 2 times **more**, then repeat from † to † once, sc in same st as first sc; join with slip st to first sc: 748 sts.

Rnd 3: Ch 1, 3 sc in same st, † sc in next 5 sts, 3 sc in next dtr, (sc in next 9 sts, 3 sc in next dtr) 14 times, sc in next 5 sts, 3 sc in next sc, sc in next 5 sts, 3 sc in next dtr, (sc in next 9 sts, 3 sc in next dtr) 21 times, sc in next 5 sts †, 3 sc in next sc, repeat from † to † once; join with slip st to first sc, finish off.

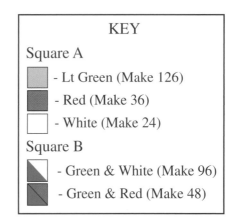

KEY
Square A
⬜ - Lt Green (Make 126)
⬛ - Red (Make 36)
⬜ - White (Make 24)
Square B
◿ - Green & White (Make 96)
◿ - Green & Red (Make 48)

Warm & Cuddly

This extra-cuddly afghan will be everyone's best friend on cold winter nights! The diamond effect is created by alternating two colors of yarn as you work with one and carry the other.

Finished Size: 50" x 65"

MATERIALS
Sport Weight Yarn:
    Spruce - 30 ounces, (850 grams, 3,000 yards)
    Off White - 25 ounces, (710 grams, 2,500 yards)
    Crochet hook, size G (4.00 mm) **or** size needed for gauge

GAUGE: 9 Star Sts and 10 rows = 4"

STITCH GUIDE

BEGINNING STAR ST
YO, insert hook in third ch from hook, YO and pull up a loop, YO, insert hook in eyelet of next Star St, YO and pull up a loop, YO and draw through all 5 loops on hook, ch 1 to close Star St and form eyelet.

STAR ST
YO, insert hook in same eyelet as last leg of last Star St made, YO and pull up a loop, YO, insert hook in eyelet of next Star St, YO and pull up a loop, YO and draw through all 5 loops on hook, ch 1 to close Star St and form eyelet.

ENDING STAR ST
YO, insert hook in same eyelet as last leg of last Star St made, YO and pull up a loop, YO, insert hook in sp **before** turning ch, YO and pull up a loop, YO and draw through all 5 loops on hook.
Note: First ch of turning ch on following row will serve as eyelet for Ending Star St.

To work **color change** at the beginning of a row, hook new yarn and draw through loop on hook, forming first ch of beginning ch-3. To change color within a row, work Star St indicated to within one step of completion (one loop on hook), hook new yarn, and draw through loop on hook, forming ch-1 eyelet. Work over unused color, holding yarn with normal tension and keeping it to **wrong** side of work.

AFGHAN BODY
With Spruce, ch 221 **loosely**, place marker in third ch from hook for st placement.

Row 1 (Right side): YO, insert hook in third ch from hook, YO and pull up a loop, YO, skip next ch, insert hook in next ch, YO and pull up a loop, YO and draw through all 5 loops on hook, ★ ch 1 to close Star St and form eyelet, YO, insert hook in same ch as last leg of Star St just made, YO and pull up a loop, YO, skip next ch, insert hook in next ch, YO and pull up a loop, YO and draw through all 5 loops on hook; repeat from ★ across: 109 Star Sts.

Row 2: Ch 1 changing to Off White, ch 2, **turn**; work Beginning Star St changing to Spruce, work 11 Star Sts changing to Off White in last st, ★ work Star St changing to Spruce, work 11 Star Sts changing to Off White in last st; repeat from ★ 7 times **more**, work Ending Star St.

Row 3: Ch 3, turn; work Beginning Star St, work Star St changing to Spruce, work 9 Star Sts changing to Off White in last st, ★ work 3 Star Sts changing to Spruce in last st, work 9 Star Sts changing to Off White in last st; repeat from ★ 7 times **more**, work Star St, work Ending Star St.

Row 4: Ch 3, turn; work Beginning Star St, work 2 Star Sts changing to Spruce in last st, work 7 Star Sts changing to Off White in last st, ★ work 5 Star Sts changing to Spruce in last st, work 7 Star Sts changing to Off White in last st; repeat from ★ 7 times **more**, work 2 Star Sts, work Ending Star St.

Row 5: Ch 3, turn; work Beginning Star St, work 3 Star Sts changing to Spruce in last st, work 5 Star Sts changing to Off White in last st, ★ work 7 Star Sts changing to Spruce in last st, work 5 Star Sts changing to Off White in last st; repeat from ★ 7 times **more**, work 3 Star Sts, work Ending Star St.

Row 6: Ch 3, turn; work Beginning Star St, work 4 Star Sts changing to Spruce in last st, work 3 Star Sts changing to Off White in last st, ★ work 9 Star Sts changing to Spruce in last st, work 3 Star Sts changing to Off White in last st; repeat from ★ 7 times **more**, work 4 Star Sts, work Ending Star St.

Continued on page 132.

Row 7: Ch 3, turn; work Beginning Star St, work 5 Star Sts changing to Spruce in last st, work Star St changing to Off White, ★ work 11 Star Sts changing to Spruce in last st, work Star St changing to Off White; repeat from ★ 7 times **more**, work 5 Star Sts, work Ending Star St.

Row 8: Ch 3, turn; work Beginning Star St, work 4 Star Sts changing to Spruce in last st, work 3 Star Sts changing to Off White in last st, ★ work 9 Star Sts changing to Spruce in last st, work 3 Star Sts changing to Off White in last st; repeat from ★ 7 times **more**, work 4 Star Sts, work Ending Star St.

Row 9: Ch 3, turn; work Beginning Star St, work 3 Star Sts changing to Spruce in last st, work 5 Star Sts changing to Off White in last st, ★ work 7 Star Sts changing to Spruce in last st, work 5 Star Sts changing to Off White in last st; repeat from ★ 7 times **more**, work 3 Star Sts, work Ending Star St.

Row 10: Ch 3, turn; work Beginning Star St, work 2 Star Sts changing to Spruce in last st, work 7 Star Sts changing to Off White in last st, ★ work 5 Star Sts changing to Spruce in last st, work 7 Star Sts changing to Off White in last st; repeat from ★ 7 times **more**, work 2 Star Sts, work Ending Star St.

Row 11: Ch 3, turn; work Beginning Star St, work Star St changing to Spruce, work 9 Star Sts changing to Off White in last st, ★ work 3 Star Sts changing to Spruce in last st, work 9 Star Sts changing to Off White in last st; repeat from ★ 7 times **more**, work Star St, work Ending Star St.

Row 12: Ch 3, turn; work Beginning Star St changing to Spruce, work 11 Star Sts changing to Off White in last st, ★ work Star St changing to Spruce, work 11 Star Sts changing to Off White in last st; repeat from ★ 7 times **more**, work Ending Star St.

Row 13: Ch 1 changing to Spruce, ch 2, **turn**; work Beginning Star St, work Star Sts across, work Ending Star St.

Rows 14-157: Repeat Rows 2-13, 12 times; do **not** finish off.
Cut Off White.

EDGING

Rnd 1: Ch 2, do **not** turn; 2 sc in second ch from hook, work 283 sc evenly spaced across end of rows; working in free loops of beginning ch *(Fig. 17b, page 141)*, 3 sc in first ch, work 217 sc evenly spaced across to marked ch, 3 sc in marked ch; work 283 sc evenly spaced across end of rows; working across Row 157, 3 sc in top of turning ch, work 217 sc evenly spaced across, sc in same st as first sc; join with slip st to first sc: 1012 sc.

Rnd 2: Ch 3 **(counts as first dc)**, 3 dc in same st, ★ † skip next sc, sc in next sc, (skip next 2 sc, 6 dc in next sc, skip next 2 sc, sc in next sc) across to within one sc of center sc of next corner 3-sc group, skip next sc †, 8 dc in center sc; repeat from ★ 2 times **more**, then repeat from † to † once, 4 dc in same st as first dc; join with slip st to first dc, finish off.

Winter Melody

Two harmonious hues make beautiful music together on this tempting throw.
The soft accent will complement any room with its comforting warmth.

Finished Size: 48" x 61^1/$_2$"

MATERIALS

Worsted Weight Yarn:
    Dk Green - 38 ounces, (1,080 grams, 2,615 yards)
    Green - 4 ounces, (110 grams, 275 yards)
Crochet hook, size H (5.00 mm) **or** size needed for
    gauge
Yarn needle

GAUGE: Each Strip = 4" wide
               8 rows = 4"

Gauge Swatch: 2^1/$_4$"w x 4"h
Work same as Strip Center through Row 8.

STITCH GUIDE

> **LONG SINGLE CROCHET**
> *(abbreviated LSC)*
> Working **around** next ch-1 *(Fig. 18, page 140)*,
> insert hook in **both** loops of sc one row **below**
> ch-1, YO and pull up a loop even with last st
> made, YO and draw through both loops on
> hook *(Fig. 9, page 139)*.

STRIP (Make 12)
CENTER

With Dk Green, ch 14 **loosely**.

Row 1: Dc in fifth ch from hook, skip next 2 chs, sc
in next ch, ch 2, skip next 2 chs, sc in next ch, skip
next 2 chs, (dc, ch 1, dc) in last ch: 5 sts and 3 sps.

Row 2 (Right side): Ch 1, turn; sc in first dc, skip
next ch-1 sp, 5 dc in next ch-2 sp, skip next 2 sts and
next ch, sc in next ch: 7 sts.

Note: Loop a short piece of yarn around any stitch
to mark Row 2 as **right** side and bottom edge.

Row 3: Ch 4 **(counts as first dc plus ch 1)**, turn; dc
in same st, skip next dc, sc in next dc, ch 2, skip next
dc, sc in next dc, skip next dc, (dc, ch 1, dc) in last
sc: 6 sts and 3 sps.

Row 4: Ch 1, turn; sc in first dc, skip next ch-1 sp,
5 dc in next ch-2 sp, skip next 2 sts and next ch, sc in
last dc: 7 sts.

Rows 5-116: Repeat Rows 3 and 4, 56 times; do **not**
finish off.

BORDER

Rnd 1: Ch 1, do **not** turn; working in end of rows, sc
in first row, ch 3, skip next row, (sc in next row, ch 3,
skip next row) across; working in free loops of
beginning ch *(Fig. 17b, page 141)*, sc in ch at base of
first dc, ch 3, skip next 2 chs, sc in next ch, ch 4, skip
next 2 chs, sc in next ch, ch 3, skip next 2 chs, sc in
last ch, ch 3; working in end of rows, skip first row,
sc in next row, ch 3, (skip next row, sc in next row,
ch 3) across; working in sts on Row 116, skip first sc,
sc in next dc, ch 4, skip next 3 dc, sc in next dc, ch 3;
join with slip st to first sc, finish off: 122 sps.

Rnd 2: With **right** side facing, join Green with sc in
ch-3 sp **before** joining *(see Joining With Sc,
page 140)*; 2 sc in same sp, ch 1, ★ (3 sc in next
ch-3 sp, ch 1) across to next ch-4 sp, 5 dc in ch-4 sp,
ch 1; repeat from ★ once **more**; join with slip st to
Back Loop Only of first sc *(Fig. 16, page 141)*,
finish off: 370 sts and 122 ch-1 sps.

Rnd 3: With **right** side facing and working in Back
Loop Only of sts on Rnd 2, join Dk Green with sc in
same st as joining; sc in next 2 sc, † work LSC, (sc in
next 3 sc, work LSC) across to within 3 sc of next
5-dc group, sc in next 3 sc, skip next ch-1 sp, sc in
next 2 dc, (sc, ch 1, sc) in next dc †, sc in next 2 dc,
skip next ch-1 sp, sc in next 3 sc, repeat from † to †
once, sc in last 2 dc; join with slip st to **both** loops of
first sc, finish off.

ASSEMBLY

With Dk Green and working through inside loops
only, whipstitch long edge of Strips together
(Fig. 21a, page 142), beginning in first LSC and
ending in last LSC.

EDGING

With **right** side facing and working across long edge, join Dk Green with sc in first LSC; † (ch 2, skip next sc, sc in next st) across to within 2 sc of next ch-1 sp, ch 3, skip next 2 sc, (sc, ch 3) twice in next ch-1 sp, ★ skip next 2 sc, (sc in next sc, ch 2, skip next sc) twice, pull up a loop in same st as joining on same Strip and in same st as joining on next Strip, YO and draw through all 3 loops on hook, (ch 2, skip next sc, sc in next sc) twice, ch 3, skip next 2 sc, (sc, ch 3) twice in next ch-1 sp; repeat from ★ 10 times **more**, skip next 2 sc †, sc in next sc, repeat from † to † once, (sc in next sc, ch 2, skip next sc) twice; join with slip st to first sc, finish off.

ABBREVIATIONS

BLO	Back Loop(s) Only	FPtr	Front Post treble crochet(s)
BP	Back Post	hdc	half double crochet(s)
BPdc	Back Post double crochet(s)	LDC	Long double crochet(s)
BPtr	Back Post treble crochet(s)	LSC	Long single crochet(s)
ch(s)	chain(s)	Lt	Light
dc	double crochet(s)	mm	millimeters
Dk	Dark	Rnd(s)	Round(s)
dtr	double treble crochet(s)	sc	single crochet(s)
FLO	Front Loop(s) Only	sp(s)	space(s)
FP	Front Post	st(s)	stitch(es)
FPdc	Front Post double crochet(s)	tr	treble crochet(s)
FPhdc	Front Post half double crochet(s)	YO	yarn over

★ — work instructions following ★ as many **more** times as indicated in addition to the first time.

† to † or ♥ to ♥ — work all instructions from first † to second † or from first ♥ to second ♥ **as many** times as specified.

( ) or [ ] — work enclosed instructions **as many** times as specified by the number immediately following **or** work all enclosed instructions in the stitch or space indicated **or** contains explanatory remarks.

colon (:) — the number(s) given after a colon at the end of a row or round denote(s) the number of stitches you should have on that row or round.

TERMS

chain loosely — work the chain **only** loose enough for the hook to pass through the chain easily when working the next row or round into the chain.

leg — the first or second part of a pattern stitch.

post — the vertical shaft of a stitch.

right side vs. wrong side — the right side of your work is the side that will show when the piece is finished.

work across or around — continue working in the established pattern.

GAUGE

Gauge is the number of stitches and rows or rounds per inch and is used to determine the finished size of an Afghan. All patterns in this book specify the gauge that you must match to ensure proper size and to ensure that you will have enough yarn to complete your Afghan.

Hook size given in instructions is merely a guide. Because everyone crochets differently — loosely, tightly, or somewhere in between — the finished size can vary, even when crocheters use the very same pattern, yarn, and hook.

Before beginning your Afghan, it is absolutely necessary for you to crochet a gauge swatch in the pattern stitch indicated and with the weight of yarn and hook size suggested. Your swatch must be large enough to measure your gauge. Lay your swatch on a hard, smooth, flat surface. Then measure it, counting your stitches and rows or rounds carefully. If your swatch is smaller than specified or you have too many stitches per inch, try again with a larger size hook; if your swatch is larger than specified or you don't have enough stitches per inch, try again with a smaller size hook. Keep trying until you find the size that will give you the specified gauge. **DO NOT HESITATE TO CHANGE HOOK SIZE TO OBTAIN CORRECT GAUGE.** Once proper gauge is obtained, measure the width of the Afghan approximately every 3" to be sure gauge remains consistent.

BASIC STITCH GUIDE

CHAIN *(abbreviated ch)*

To work a chain stitch, begin with a slip knot on the hook. Bring the yarn **over** the hook from **back** to **front**, catching the yarn with the hook and turning the hook slightly toward you to keep the yarn from slipping off. Draw the yarn through the slip knot *(Fig. 1)*.

Fig. 1

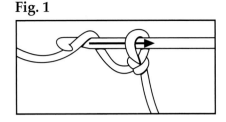

WORKING INTO THE CHAIN

When beginning a first row of crochet in a chain, always skip the first chain from the hook and work into the second chain from hook (for single crochet), third chain from hook (for half double crochet), or fourth chain from hook (for double crochet), etc. *(Fig. 2a)*.

Fig. 2a

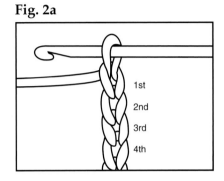

1st
2nd
3rd
4th

Method 1: Insert hook into back ridge of each chain indicated *(Fig. 2b)*.
Method 2: Insert hook under top loop **and** the back ridge of each chain indicated *(Fig. 2c)*.

Fig. 2b **Fig. 2c**

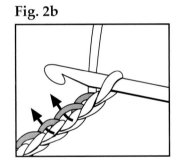
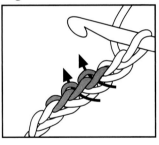

SLIP STITCH *(abbreviated slip st)*

This stitch is used to attach new yarn, to join work, or to move the yarn across a group of stitches without adding height.
Insert hook in stitch or space indicated, YO and draw through stitch **and** loop on hook *(Fig. 3)*.

Fig. 3

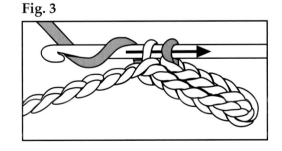

SINGLE CROCHET *(abbreviated sc)*

Insert hook in stitch or space indicated, YO and pull up a loop, YO and draw through both loops on hook *(Fig. 4)*.

Fig. 4

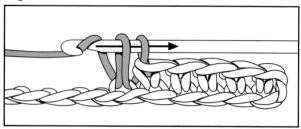

HALF DOUBLE CROCHET

(abbreviated hdc)

YO, insert hook in stitch or space indicated, YO and pull up a loop, YO and draw through all 3 loops on hook *(Fig. 5)*.

Fig. 5

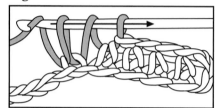

DOUBLE CROCHET *(abbreviated dc)*

YO, insert hook in stitch or space indicated, YO and pull up a loop (3 loops on hook), YO and draw through 2 loops on hook *(Fig. 6a)*, YO and draw through remaining 2 loops on hook *(Fig. 6b)*.

Fig. 6a

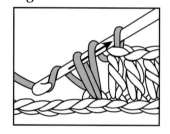

Fig. 6b

TREBLE CROCHET *(abbreviated tr)*

YO twice, insert hook in stitch or space indicated, YO and pull up a loop (4 loops on hook) *(Fig. 7a)*, (YO and draw through 2 loops on hook) 3 times *(Fig. 7b)*.

Fig. 7a

Fig. 7b

DOUBLE TREBLE CROCHET

(abbreviated dtr)

YO 3 times, insert hook in stitch or space indicated, YO and pull up a loop (5 loops on hook) *(Fig. 8a)*, (YO and draw through 2 loops on hook) 4 times *(Fig. 8b)*.

Fig. 8a

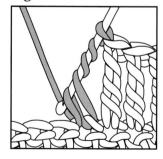

Fig. 8b

PATTERN STITCHES

LONG STITCH

Work single crochet (sc) or double crochet (dc), inserting hook in stitch or space indicated in instructions *(Fig. 9)*, and pulling up a loop even with loop on hook; complete stitch.

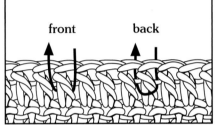
Fig. 9

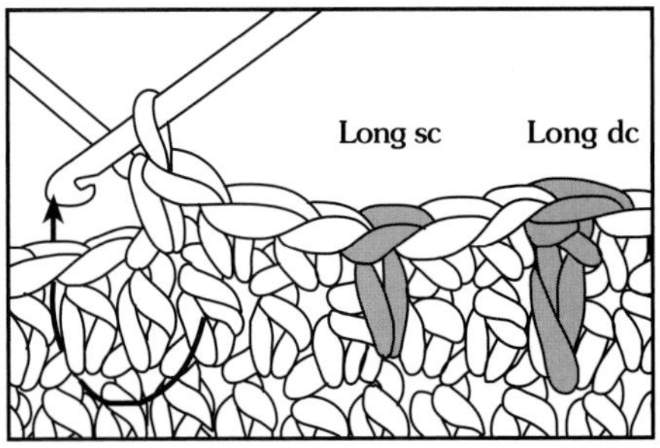

Long sc   Long dc

POST STITCH

Work around post of stitch indicated, inserting hook in direction of arrow *(Fig. 10)*.

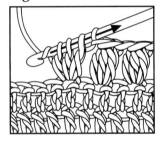
Fig. 10

front   back

CLUSTER

A Cluster can be worked all in the same stitch or space *(Figs. 11a & b)*, **or** across several stitches *(Figs. 12a & b)*.

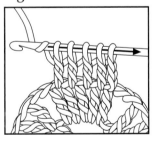
Fig. 11a

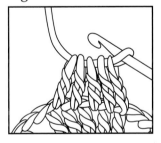
Fig. 11b

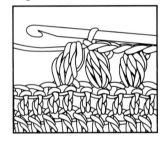
Fig. 12a

Fig. 12b

PUFF STITCH

★ YO, insert hook in stitch or space indicated, YO and pull up a loop even with loop on hook; repeat from ★ as many times as specified, YO and draw through all loops on hook *(Fig. 13)*.

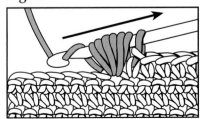
Fig. 13

POPCORN

Work specified number of dc in stitch or space indicated, drop loop from hook, insert hook in first dc of dc group, hook dropped loop and draw through *(Fig. 14)*.

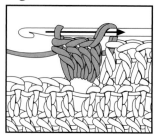

Fig. 14

REVERSE SINGLE CROCHET

(abbreviated reverse sc)

Working from **left** to **right**, insert hook in stitch to right of hook *(Fig. 15a)*, YO and draw through, under and to left of loop on hook (2 loops on hook) *(Fig. 15b)*. YO and draw through both loops on hook *(Fig. 15c)* *(reverse sc made, Fig. 15d)*.

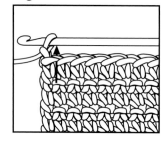

Fig. 15a

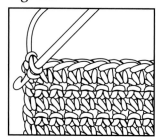

Fig. 15b

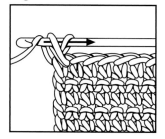

Fig. 15c

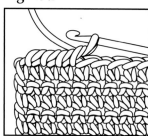

Fig. 15d

STITCHING TIPS

MARKERS

Markers are used to help distinguish the right side of the Afghan **or** to identify a specific stitch to be worked into later. Place a 2" scrap piece of yarn around a stitch on the row or round indicated, removing the marker after the Afghan is completed **or** as indicated in the instructions.

JOINING WITH SC

When instructed to join with sc, begin with a slip knot on hook. Insert hook in stitch or space indicated, YO and pull up a loop, YO and draw through both loops on hook.

JOINING WITH DC

When instructed to join with dc, begin with a slip knot on hook. YO, holding loop on hook, insert hook in stitch or space indicated, YO and pull up a loop (3 loops on hook), (YO and draw through 2 loops on hook) twice.

BACK OR FRONT LOOP ONLY
Work only in loop(s) indicated by arrow *(Fig. 16)*.

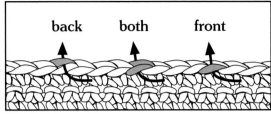
Fig. 16

FREE LOOPS
After working in Back or Front Loops Only on a row or round, there will be a ridge of unused loops. These are called the free loops. Later, when instructed to work in the free loops of the same row or round, work in these loops *(Fig. 17a)*.
When instructed to work in a free loop of a beginning chain, work in loop indicated by arrow *(Fig. 17b)*.

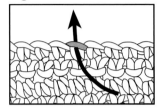
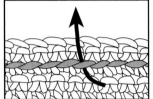
Fig. 17a   Fig. 17b

WORKING IN FRONT OF, AROUND, OR BEHIND A STITCH
Work in stitch or space indicated, inserting hook in direction of arrow *(Fig. 18)*.

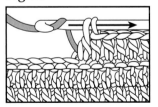
Fig. 18

CHANGING COLORS
Work the last stitch to within one step of completion, hook new yarn *(Fig. 19)* and draw through loops on hook.

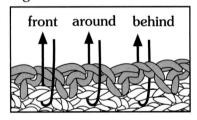
Fig. 19

WORKING IN SPACE BEFORE STITCH
When instructed to work in space **before** a stitch or in spaces **between** stitches, insert hook in space indicated by arrow *(Fig. 20)*.

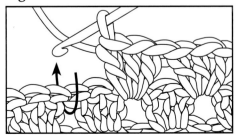
Fig. 20

FINISHING

WHIPSTITCH

With **wrong** sides together and beginning in corner stitch, sew through both pieces once to secure the beginning of the seam, leaving an ample yarn end to weave in later. Insert needle from **front** to **back** through **inside** loops of **each** piece *(Fig. 21a)* **or** through **both** loops *(Fig. 21b)*. Bring needle around and insert it from **front** to **back** through the next loops of **both** pieces. Continue in this manner across to next corner, keeping the sewing yarn fairly loose.

Fig. 21a

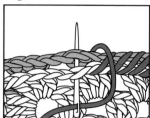

Fig. 21b

FRINGE

Cut a piece of cardboard 8" wide and half as long as strands indicated in individual instructions. Wind the yarn **loosely** and **evenly** around the length of the cardboard until the card is filled, then cut across one end; repeat as needed. Align the number of strands desired and fold in half.

With **wrong** side facing and using a crochet hook, draw the folded end up through a stitch, row, or loop, and pull the loose ends through the folded end *(Figs. 22a & b)*; draw the knot up **tightly** *(Figs. 22c & d)*. Repeat, spacing as specified. Lay flat on a hard surface and trim the ends.

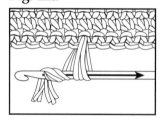

Fig. 22a

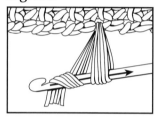

Fig. 22b

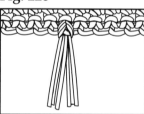

Fig. 22c

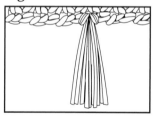

Fig. 22d

CREDITS

To Magna IV Color Imaging of Little Rock, Arkansas, we say thank you for the superb color reproduction and excellent pre-press preparation.

We want to especially thank photographers Ken West and Mark Mathews of Peerless Photography and Jerry R. Davis of Jerry Davis Photography, all of Little Rock, Arkansas, for their time, patience, and excellent work.

We would like to extend a special word of thanks to the talented designers who created the lovely projects in this book:

Eleanor Albano-Miles: *Tropical Delight*, page 51
Donna J. Barranti: *Warm & Cuddly*, page 131
Mary Lamb Becker: *Blushing Beauty*, page 30
Marilyn Buys: *Star-Spangled Banner*, page 48
Rosalie DeVries: *Vibrant Visions*, page 61
Sue Galucki: *Harvest Blend*, page 72, and *Mums Galore*, page 98
Kathleen Garen: *Home on the Range*, page 82
Anne Halliday: *Meadow*, page 8; *Stunning Stripes*, page 10; *Floral Bounty*, page 20;
    Lullaby, page 22; *Enchantment*, page 25; *Carnival*, page 64; *Sun-Baked Tiles*, page 85;
    Fall Festival, page 93; *Memories*, page 104; and *Fireside Companion*, page 126
Jan Hatfield: *Cobblestone Path*, page 6; *Veranda*, page 28; *Elegant Ivy*, page 54; and
    Spiced Tea, page 76
Terry Kimbrough: *Spring Fancy*, page 12; *Lavender & Lace*, page 46; and *Pretty in Pink*, page 58
Ann Kirtley: *Soft Clover*, page 17
Tammy Kreimeyer: *Sunrise*, page 40; *Autumn Glory*, page 88; and *Chill Chaser*, page 115
Patricia Kristoffersen: *Hospitality*, page 90
Melissa Leapman: *Reverie*, page 32; *Bride's Dream*, page 44; *Thanksgiving*, page 74;
    Log Cabin Legacy, page 80; and *Snow on the Pines*, page 106
Roberta Maier: *Hearthside Stripes*, page 110
Carole Prior: *Rock-A-Bye Blanket*, page 78, and *Remnants*, page 96
Nanette Seale: *American Spirit*, page 42
Barbara Shaffer: *Rosy Comfort*, page 66; *Tradition*, page 118; *Pretty Poinsettias*, page 120;
    and *Icicles*, page 123
Georgia A. Shaulis: *Fall Breeze*, page 100
Mary Ann Sipes: *Dazzling Dahlias*, page 68
Teresa Smith: *Idyllic Day*, page 56; *Cozy Classic*, page 108; and *Winter Melody*, page 134
Martha Brooks Stein: *Viola Patch*, page 14, and *Christmas Crowns*, page 128
Gail Tanquary: *Angels All Around*, page 112
Kim Wiltfang: *Picturesque Posies*, page 34